I thoroughly enjoyed th   )ok.
They both challenged ar   was
reminded again of the v   vays
God speaks into our lives. The testimonies within these pages truly are, to
borrow a phrase from Jerry Pattengale, "unexpected gifts." I hope they are
for others as well.

—Stacy Hammons, provost of Indiana Wesleyan University

I love this book. It's full of inspiration, encouragement, and a realistic look at
life from a Christian perspective. The authors have captured everyday life
through the stories of people who sit in the pew without others knowing what
they are dealing with each day. My faith was increased and my heart warmed
after reading this book. I highly recommend that pastors and churches
purchase large quantities of the book to distribute to church leaders. I believe
it will increase sensitivity to the needs of those in the church, raise the faith
level of any person who reads its pages, as well as increase compassionate
outreach to the community in which they minister.

—Stan Toler, bestselling author and speaker

There is nothing more riveting than a good story that reveals the heart of
God for his children. This wonderful collection inspires, convicts, teaches,
and reminds us of God's goodness and kindness. It is profoundly moving
to read and will be a gift to share.

—Emilie Wierda, president of Eagle Companies

The everyday stories recounted herein represent diverse voices, which
makes this collection relatable and refreshing. Simultaneously, these voices
are uniformly authentic, which is hardly an "everyday" phenomenon, and
thus makes this collection powerful and challenging as well.

—Jeff Zurcher, executive director of The Arington Foundation

FAITH MADE REAL

EVERYDAY EXPERIENCES OF GOD'S POWER

Edited by Jerry Pattengale
with Steve DeNeff and Emily Vermilya

wesleyan
PUBLISHING HOUSE
wphstore.com
Fishers, IN

Copyright © 2017 by College Wesleyan Church
Published by Wesleyan Publishing House
Indianapolis, Indiana 46250
Printed in the United States of America
ISBN: 978-1-63257-120-5
ISBN (e-book): 978-1-63257-121-2

Library of Congress Cataloging-in-Publication Data
Pattengale, Jerry A., editor.
Faith made real : everyday experiences of God's power / Jerry Pattengale, general
  editor, with Steve DeNeff and Emily Vermilya.
Indianapolis : Wesleyan Publishing House, 2017.
LCCN 2016053417 (print) | LCCN 2016055104 (ebook) | ISBN 9781632571205 (pbk.)
  | ISBN 9781632571212 (e-book)
LCSH: God (Christianity)--Faithfulness. | Providence and government of God--
  Christianity. | Christian life--Anecdotes.
LCC BT103 .F35 2017 (print) | LCC BT103 (ebook) | DDC   231.7--dc23LC record
  available at https://lccn.loc.gov/2016053417

CONTENTS

Free shepherding resources are available at
www.wphresources.com/faithmadereal.

FOREWORD

In response to God's promise and calling in Psalm 78:3–7, we share this treasury of true stories. While some of them are embedded in tragedy and great loss, they are also immersed in great wonder and joy in the midst of finding God's faithfulness. Special thanks to Jerry Pattengale, who has been a part of College Wesleyan Church for more than three decades, and selflessly collected all these stories without any financial compensation. Also, our gratitude to the people of College Wesleyan Church who, with great courage, shared glimpses into their personal journeys and some of what God is doing in their lives. They are living proof that miracles still happen and real transformation is possible in the lives of ordinary people.

As you read, we hope you are inspired, encouraged, and even surprised; but mostly filled with great hope. And wherever you may find yourself, be assured that you are part of God's great story.

O my people, listen to my teaching. Open your ears to what I am saying. For I will show you lessons from our history, stories handed down to us from former generations. I will reveal these truths to you so that you can describe these glorious deeds of Jehovah to your children and tell them about the mighty miracles he did. For he gave his laws to Israel and commanded our fathers to teach them to their children, so that they in turn could teach their children too. Thus his laws pass down from generation to generation. In this way each generation has been able to obey his laws and to set its hope anew on God and not forget his glorious miracles.

—Psalm 78:1–7 (TLB)

INTRODUCTION

Most of us love engaging stories, especially about real people and actual events. The church is no exception.

Though most of my career has revolved around publishing, it took me twenty years to gain the courage to write parts of my story. My childhood poverty embarrassed me. How would publishers of my academic work react to tales of life with my alcoholic father and renegade relatives? Would my most cherished memories and heartfelt lessons make any difference in the lives of readers? I basically wanted some guarantee that my honesty was worth the risk. However, there is no guarantee, and those contributing to this book realize that we trust our work to God alone. We write with prudence but also become personally vulnerable.

Publishing personal reflections in any form certainly wasn't part of my career plan and perhaps could submarine vocational possibilities. But when God called me to transparency, not for my sake but for others', the articles, now numbering more than 250, began. I soon found great fulfillment in the process, but the first few were especially painful and agonizing to write. I know many contributors in this book join me in taking a step toward transparency.

Early on, perhaps I wasn't ready, or mature enough, to share personal material. Whatever the reason, I lacked the courage to talk about my childhood in the backwaters of Buck Creek, Indiana. But during the past two decades, these stories seem to have resonated with audiences ranging from the *Chicago Tribune* readers to editors at McGraw-Hill. People like to laugh, and at times cry, as they relate to someone's journey. Themes such as "unexpected gifts" have uplifted readers. I think of the story about our family of ten finding our lawn covered with presents on Christmas Eve. Or "embarrassment," the day I swished a thirty-foot jumper in a packed Hoosier gymnasium . . . into the wrong goal. Or dealing with loss, failures, or impatience. But I've also written of God's provision, such as the day during grad school when I prayed for two dollars to buy drinks at lunchtimes until payday. I got off my knees, and while walking to the car I found two dollars in my yard. Yes, I should have prayed for a million. And yes, it was a moment that sustained me through many times of trial.

In reality, each local church is filled with similar stories of people's unique highs and lows, of their histories, and, more important, of God's faithfulness and providence—the miraculous among the seemingly mundane.

The same is true of your church, wherever you attend. We've entered an era in which "reality" is captivating listeners. Not all people are ready to share their stories, at least not alone. Some need help articulating a glimpse into their journeys. I've been asked to assist with that in this collection. Others who share in this book, however, are brilliant communicators and could help most of us with our own stories. One of the contributors in the following pages has authored dozens of books over a lifetime of celebrated leadership. Another is a coauthor and illustrator of two *New York Times* bestsellers, in addition to hundreds of other book projects. Yet for many, this is a first venture into public disclosure—which is a key element of this book's special appeal. Whether in Buck Creek, Baltimore, or Burbank, we all have learned lessons along the way.

Members from any single church represent assorted gifts and stories. Their life situations—whether by choice, accident, inheritance, or surroundings—bring a variety of different perspectives. From stories of redemption and restoration, to saintly lifestyles and selfless neighbors, we find our way more easily in such light. Think about those with whom you worship, those who greet you at the church doors or work in the church offices. Reflect on conversations you've had with church janitors, youth pastors, or board members. All of them have journeys that helped inform their spiritual lives and likely yours.

I've spent nearly thirty years in the church where the authors of these stories attend. Some of the written recollections introduced me to these meaningful aspects of their journeys. Although I was familiar with several of the writers' histories, their articulation of key episodes from their lives enriched mine. My hope is that this project encourages you to gather stories from those with whom you worship. And perhaps to learn the biggest lesson I learned in this editing process: to be more observant to the real-life stories already before you.

—Jerry Pattengale

PART 1

THE **TRUTH**
OF **GODLY**
INFLUENCE

A COMMUNAL ADVENTURE
THE SPIRITUAL DISCIPLINE OF HOSPITALITY

ERIN CRISP

Editor's Note: *Few things would tax me more than sharing a house long-term with another family, let alone splitting its mortgage. Before getting married, I lived for almost two years alone in a two-room cabin near Glendora, California. No phone, radio, or TV. Even the entrance to the area had a security gate. Though I love people, and most friends know me as a socialite and (I think) a lot of fun, the truth is that I crave my quiet space.*

Against this backdrop, Erin's story prompted me to think about the benefits of communal living, if only for a season, and to ponder a fuller view of biblical hospitality and community. Most of our friends can sit around our dinner table and swap stories of those tough young adult years. Of using a card table and folding chairs until real furniture was affordable. Of the old AMC Pacer or Impala that somehow kept running long after it looked drivable. Of knowing the cupboards were bare when unexpected visitors dropped by. Erin's journey has that, but a whole lot more. Except for college dorms and church camps, it's an experience I'll likely never have, but one I've enjoyed catching a glimpse of from afar.

▼ ▼ ▼

I was twenty-five years old and life seemed picture perfect. Our three boys were happy and healthy, ages six, three, and one and a half. I worked part time as the children's ministry director at the church where my husband, Eric, served as youth pastor. I brought my baby to work with me most days, and in every way we had all that we needed and more. In my heart of hearts though, I was bored. Is this it? Is this the Christian life: women's Bible studies, craft bazaars, scrapbooking, and house parties of every variety? Participating in church activities—it seemed like the ministry-spouse thing to do.

Fast-forward eight months, and Eric and I sold our home and half of our belongings. We moved to Wilmore, Kentucky, for seminary, leaving all of our extended family and security behind. I felt alive again. Finances and friendships weren't easy, and neither was establishing a new normal. But I was hungering and thirsting after God's presence in life-giving ways.

We hit it off with two couples that we welcomed into our tiny living room every Sunday evening—eating, laughing, and learning together, for long, fulfilling hours.

When these new friends stopped by unannounced, I didn't scurry with embarrassed attempts to clean up. They saw our house dirty, our kids angry, my hair messy, and our lives in all seasons. They even used our washer and dryer. When they received the call that a parent had died unexpectedly and tragically, we were together folding laundry.

Eric and I recognized the work God was doing in us as we opened up to authentic relationships. God revealed my pride, self-centeredness, impatience, distrust, and insecurity as I submitted to the Father of Christian community. I wanted more. We sold our home once again and bought a house with one of the couples—all four of us on the mortgage.

In the process of moving in together, we wanted our home to continue to be a place of hospitality. Hadn't hospitality originally brought our little group together? And every time we opened up to others, God blessed our own lives. We were hooked. We all committed to keep at least one bedroom of this new home open and available for others.

During the two years we lived together, we hosted some special guests. Mr. Stephen, a Nigerian ministry student, stayed for one year. Others hailed from Lebanon and Kenya. Several travelers stayed for a week, attending intensive classes or conferences. Every guest was a blessing in one way or another. We usually say that people are a blessing when they give us something—they cook us a meal or write us an encouraging note. But my definition was expanding.

Mr. Stephen hadn't seen his son, still back in Kenya, for nearly two years. When he showed me a photo of his son, who had been given a birthday present of three small glass bottles of soda and a used baseball cap, he blessed me. He provided a living, breathing mirror that reflected my own excessive relationship to my possessions. It wasn't shame or guilt that I felt (OK—maybe a little shame) but rather the glaring awareness of the Holy Spirit. Eric and I reevaluated "things" in our lives.

Such glimpses into my soul would sometimes cascade like a flood until I was gasping, "OK, enough, God. I get it. I need more of you." And so this became my daily plea. I took walks often and breathed this prayer while I inhaled, "More of you, God" and exhaled "Less of me." I literally inflated my lungs with God's goodness and mercy and breathed out the selfishness he was revealing in my soul. Was it easy to confront my own sinful nature? No. Was it a blessing? Absolutely.

Today these precious house-sharing friends remain closer to us than family. We live in separate states and speak to one another only a few times each year, but we always spend a summer week together, our times as sweet and rich as ever.

So what has been the long-term impact? Eric and I don't live communally anymore (although Eric's parents live with us for part of the year), but the remnants of those times remain. Extraordinary hospitality transformed my soul. I don't waste opportunities to deepen friendships. I don't worry as much about oversharing, and I don't second-guess my actions. No more, "I should've said. . . . Why didn't I say . . . ?"

I wasn't cured of selfishness, materialism, or self-criticism. They still occasionally nip at my heels, but I think they're more recognizable. After a taste of what deep community feels like—the beauty of shared laughter and tears, the unconditional love—there is new value in gathering together with God's people.

Because of my time in our "commune," I am more aware that we are all flawed and we need one another. We need much more than lectures or contrived accountability. We need genuine friendships, where real people with real needs show their vulnerability. We need to offer even the little we have to one another and accept offers of help. We need to ask tough questions and listen carefully to others' stories. We need to need one another, because where there is opportunity to show love, there is greater opportunity to receive it.

HE'S BEEN FAITHFUL
A SONG FOR MY LIFE AND MY FUNERAL

TERRI SMITH

Editor's Note: *Sometimes we read a refreshing piece and try to determine if it's the story, the style, or both that prompts our reflective smile. Not everyone has the ability to satirize the mundane like Erasmus, describe intriguing scenes like Dorothy Sayers, or draw us to the page like Harper Lee. For most of us, just glimpses of such success would be fulfilling— not for our sake but for that of our readers. Below is a reflection pointed in that creative direction, from a church member who didn't even begin college until nearly forty years of age. Terri Smith gives a punchy appraisal of her journey. It's replete with honest notions of being human in the presence of the divine and of recognizing departures in our actions from our deeply held attitudes. She invites us to think about the music that would best capture our lives at our funeral, no less. For her, it's a song by Carol Cymbala, who helped her husband build the Brooklyn Tabernacle: herself a self-taught choir director of considerable fame. I'm not sure what my funeral song will be, but Terri got me thinking about it. And more important, I'm trying to identify a song that best captures my long walk with my Savior.*

Throughout this book, we peek at similar worries and self-perceptions from some amazing people. In each case, we learn a bit more about not taking outward appearances or accomplishments for granted. If I were to ask Terri's husband, Mark, long recognized as a master teacher at his college, his opinion about this chapter, I'm reasonably sure Dr. Smith would quickly inform me that for decades he's realized who the real master teacher is in the family, with or without her degree.

▼   ▼   ▼

Getting older surprised me. Gray hair came first, then thyroid issues. Getting down on the floor is a cinch; getting back up ain't pretty. You must never ever look in a twelve-times magnifying mirror, and don't, for heaven's sake, try to jump rope anymore: the shock absorbers you once had don't, well, absorb.

But those are the physical surprises. One of the biggest wonders for me has been both delightful and sobering. It is perspective: looking back on more than forty years of belonging to Jesus. It's something like the view from the top of a mountain or down a very long stretch of highway that lies behind. You can catch the glimpse while sitting at the wedding of one of your children or at the funeral of someone dear. You're seeing with a bit more clarity the big picture of life with a bit more clarity.

My husband and I joke about all the songs he wants at his funeral. It's going to be a mix of movie theme songs, Lennon-McCartney collaborations, and great hymns of the church; it's also going to last for hours.

I have my own list, along with the people I'd like to sing. Close to the top is a song written by Carol Cymbala, "He's Been Faithful." Nearly twenty years ago, I heard it for the first time, and I marveled at the way it portrays my life in Christ. I thought of the song as I've recently been reading through my journals that chronicle life's ups and downs, victories and defeats, heartbreaks and unimaginable joys. "He's Been Faithful," with its references to so much of my own Christian life—fear and pain, weakness and despair, doubt and prayerlessness, selfishness and faithlessness—celebrates the goodness, greatness, miraculousness, utter devotion, and faithfulness of God. That song echoed in my mind as I read and remembered:

> In my moments of fear,
> through every pain, every tear,
> there's a God who's been faithful to me.[1]

I open the journals and recall when I entered the hospital to have our second child, with Isaiah 41:10 committed to my memory because of the fear of childbirth. Trembling as I changed into the hospital gown, I recited the words. The Lord Jesus filled that little bathroom with his presence and removed the fear. He also granted my request for a quick labor. Just a little more than two hours later, I held our second daughter.

I remember vividly, at age eighteen, telling my father that I was not going to college; I just didn't want to. Underneath my defiance was the fear of failing. God patiently and kindly broke through all that insecurity, and I stepped onto a college campus nearly two decades later, as a thirty-seven-year-old student. I made no promises and God made no demands. Just being there demonstrated his faithfulness to me.

For about thirty years, I battled irritable bowel syndrome (IBS). I saw family doctors and a specialist, and tried all that might help, but to no avail. I begged God to take it away. When he didn't, I abandoned hope of ever getting better. However, in the process, I began to thank him for it, because it kept me dependent on him. He gave me strength to endure and sixteen years ago, it disappeared.

The journal pages turn. Marriage is difficult at times, and ours has been no exception. Children can break your hearts, and ours did. Depression, like one of the Harry Potter Death Eaters, sucked out of me joy and the desire to live. We've now been married forty-one years, our children give us great joy—as do the grandchildren—and my heart again sings for the sheer delight of a restored mind.

One memory invites me to linger: Our destination was Wilmore, Kentucky; my husband (Mark) was starting seminary in the fall of 1982. We traveled down in May to see if we could secure a place to live, a place I had prayed repeatedly would be near enough for Mark to walk to classes because we had only one car. We found a trailer and my heart sank. It wasn't exactly what I had in mind, but it was one block from the school. So we paid our deposit, and I tried to be grateful. Before we headed back to Wilmore in July, a group of people from First Wesleyan Church in Chillicothe, Ohio, banded together, promising to pay our rent for the two years until Mark got that degree.

God has promised his presence, and he's shown up at gravesides and in hospital rooms and in the everyday stuff of life, teaching me to love and accept our non-Christian son-in-law and taking care of our disabled grandson. God strengthened me in a very tangible way when I walked through a situation fraught with hurt and distress, when he spoke through the apostle Paul, "Conduct yourselves in a manner worthy of the gospel of Christ" (Phil. 1:27). I didn't hear those words as a command; instead, God spoke them gently, reminding me that he had made me worthy and that my baby steps in him brought delight.

My father rejected our first grandchild and wouldn't speak to our daughter. Our grandson, you see, is biracial. Long years of bias surfaced as Dad raged against a marriage, and then the child born from it. But one day, three and a half years after Brady's birth, we came home from church during a visit to our hometown in Ohio, and there at the head of the table was Dad—talking to, playing with, and feeding Brady. If ever there was an impossible in my life, there it was: my father's heart changed, literally overnight, by a faithful God.

I recently heard someone say that when you become a Christian, your greatest sins could still be ahead of you. And that was true of me. Still, though I was, and am, faithless and disobedient and wandering, I've found myself pursued. It makes no sense in our bottom-line, greatest-maximum-effect world. All I can say is that the best of shepherds did a Luke 15: he sought me out and brought me home.

I met with God most mornings on the sofa. But even when I couldn't pray, Jesus drew me in. I was losing my best friend and our biggest cheer-leader; my mother-in-law, Jane, was dying. I went to that couch with tears during those days and the Spirit of Jesus whispered, "Just come sit with me." One morning, the Spirit stopped me as I read Paul's words in Romans 8:18: "I consider that our present sufferings are not worth comparing with the glory that will be revealed in us."

Later, after Jane had died, I had a dream. Jane and I were talking on the phone and the conversation was coming to an end. I told her that I loved her and she said she loved me. I told her I missed her and she did not reply. In that dream that, I think, was something a little more than a dream, I realized that God showed me the meaning of that Romans verse. She is in a place where love is still affirmed for those she loved most and not diminished by our (current) absence. The glory has been revealed. Jesus comforted me.

I am an addict, given to seeking after what makes me feel good, what I can do (sometimes so subtly that you'd never know it) to make myself feel or look good. Reading is at times an addiction. I've been known to resent setting a book aside in order to meet family demands. Then one night the Spirit clearly told me to put that desire into his hands. When I did so, reluctantly, Jesus graciously provided times to read, and I found those times so much sweeter than the ones for which I had previously grasped.

The verses in another song I want at my funeral read, "prone to wander, Lord, I feel it, prone to leave the God I love."[2] The Shepherd's sheepdogs, named *grace* and *mercy,* have nipped at my heels and nudged my sides. Some of those "sheepdogs" have other names: Mark Smith, John Stott, David Seamands, Peter Lord, Jane Smith, Glaphre Gilliland, J. I. Packer,

Craig Barnes, Tamera Rehnborg. I look beyond their words or faces, and there's Jesus, keeping me in his fold.

One particular night during a desert time, I was in bed. In my mind's eye, I lay by a tiny stream, trying to get some of the water, because I was so thirsty, so desperate, for Jesus. And then, for a few fleeting moments, the veil that separates the seen and unseen parted. I was bathed in the sense of an overwhelming love. The words that immediately came to mind as I tried to name this experience were *immense affection*. I have no explanation other than this: God came.

And so I am, as one pastor said when he was sixty years old, on the last lap of a four-lap race. I think often about the previous three laps. I reflect on life in general, on my own in particular. The chorus of "He's Been Faithful" says,

Looking back His love and mercy I see.
Though in my heart I have questioned, and failed to believe . . .[3]

So much questioning, so much unbelief! But when my life ends, when this song is sung, I also will be singing to the saints and angels (because I will finally be able to really sing), and affirming this great truth: *He's been faithful.*

NOTES

1. Carol Cymbala, "He's Been Faithful," MetroLyrics, http://www.metrolyrics.com/hes-been-faithful-lyrics-damaris-carbaugh.html.

2. Robert Robinson, "Come Thou Fount of Every Blessing," public domain.

3. Cymbala, ibid.

THE MUSIC HAS CHANGED, BUT NOT THE MESSAGE

RAY WELCH

Editor's Note: *Some people are inseparable from their life's work, and that's Ray Welch: a multifaceted musician who can play everything from the French horn and pipe organ to hand bells. He could probably write a symphony for cooking utensils if he desired; the man knows his stuff. And he's a plodder. I can't imagine him running, but then I can't imagine him standing still. He has done so much for so many and likely hopes to live another eighty years to keep teaching others. He has been a fixture in my entire history at College Wesleyan Church, which began in 1975, about forty years after he became a church member! And he has that memorable gait that hasn't changed through the decades. Always in dress clothes, always a saunter, and always that burst of energy when we meet. One side of his mouth rises with his vintage smile. He's a loyal, persistent friend, and one who has weathered many changes. Below is a vantage point that likely will resonate with many in congregations nationwide who continue to contribute, even though they've lived through major changes in their churches. For Ray, it's what remains the same that has kept him in the same church for most of his life.*

As a member of the same local church for seventy years, I've witnessed a lot of changes. Many were great, others were short-lived, and some persist to the present. During recent years, I've also realized that some changes seem to marginalize me. Perhaps it's my joining the octogenarian ranks at a church with hundreds of collegians. Maybe Bob Dylan's lyrics are more appropriate than a classical musician like me would like to admit: "The times they are a-changin.'"[1]

If you're a student, middle-aged, or even twenty years or so younger than this old concert organist, try to envision the cultural cave that I've slowly seen close around me. Imagine a day when what you enjoy now on Sundays no longer exists—or only in remote places or in services with doctrinal practices incongruous with your own. Imagine a few decades from now when there (possibly) are no worship choruses sung. No songs on PowerPoint. No electric guitars. A time when Chris Tomlin is shelved in the same manner as George Beverly Shea, the voice of the Billy Graham crusades. It's a wonder to me that Shea's once-popular rendition of "The Wonder of It All" is relatively unknown today. Think of a time when Hillsong music becomes as foreign as younger generations now find Ira Sankey songs and reel-to-reel hymn melodies. It might be all but impossible for you to imagine.

That "unimaginable" is where many of my ilk find ourselves. Million-dollar pipe organs are now collectors' items or ornamental backdrops for weddings. Many churches have carved up gorgeous woodwork to house electronic drums, or they displaced choir pews to accommodate projection equipment. Yes, "the times they are indeed a-changin.'"

There was a day when church design committees began with the central place of great musical instruments in the sanctuary. For many congregations, the "modern" organ was built into the front wall, much as the pipe organs adorned the entire upper platform; I think of the church and auditorium on the old D. L. Moody campus in Northfield, Massachusetts. From European cathedrals to the great American revival churches, both the sounds and sights were so very different from what we now experience. If you wanted to include a pipe organ in many of today's churches, you would need to poke a hole in the ceiling. Converted grocery stores and strip malls were not built as sacred space, with high ceilings reaching heavenward.

However, through all of these changes, I can smile when I count myself among other people and things that have persisted on the other side of these changes. Colleagues who have faithfully followed the Bible all their days surround my wife and me. Our old friends, and new ones also, return each Sunday to a place where the Bible is still taught as God's inerrant Word. A place where we expect to hear about miracles past, present, and future. Where orthodoxy still abounds. Where it's OK to be called a conservative. Where people are more concerned with the fruit of the Spirit than the spirit of the age.

Yes, during this sunset of my life, I've reflected on the many sunrises of the church I joined in 1949. From one lone pastor in a small brick building with a steeple, long since razed, to twenty staff members and an expansive new complex. Our new church's industrial kitchen is larger than the original church's platform. And our stand-alone JCBodyshop student ministries' facility is larger than that entire original church. It once stood a block away from the current site, known in its latter years as McConn Chapel, then used by the nearby college campus, and eventually housing McConn Coffee Shop. Finally it was flattened due to the tremendous expense of maintaining its failing foundations. But some of its stained-glass windows are strategically placed in the new campus café, named after McConn, and its stone cross sits on our church plaza. And in keeping with this tradition, our small chapel (in the new complex) contains stained glass from some of our long-time artisans, complemented by those that adorn the main sanctuary's wall.

Altar rails line the new sanctuary's platform, true to the churches of my journey. Amid the contemporary music that dominates our services, we still have a vibrant choir, grand pianos, and bell choirs. Yes, bell choirs that bless my soul.

I suppose our Wesleyan denomination, like many others, wrestles with cultural challenges, a new litany with each generation; but it still remains solidly orthodox and strongly evangelical. Our family praises God for this. My membership at College Wesleyan Church dates to 1949. At that time, I believed College Wesleyan Church was the most wonderful place—anywhere. Having grown up in small one-room churches where my father pastored, that stately brick building at the corner of Fortieth and Washington Streets near our current building complex was indeed something I practically worshiped. It was hard to separate the image of that building from its services and programs. However, what took place there during my youth did a lot for my fragile spirit.

It prepared me for what could have been a tough transition during my teen years. When my father finished college and took the pastorate in Converse, Indiana, that mecca had to be abandoned. However, other divine blessings, disguised in the move across the county, awaited, especially a consistent education. I did all four years of high school at Converse, now closed (except for the old gym), and then I returned to College Wesleyan Church when I enrolled at Marion College. My parents also moved back to Marion in 1954. Another temporary absence occurred in 1956, when I transferred to Indiana University.

With my marriage in 1961 to the amazing Wilda Grafton, I returned for the rest of my life to College Wesleyan Church; we both felt anchored there while teaching in public schools. Our boys, born in 1963 and 1966, worshiped with us into adulthood. College Wesleyan Church contributed as much to my children's spiritual development as we did as parents, and both remain devoted Christians with careers in Christian higher education.

In many ways, far beyond what space affords here to tell, the church was the center of our lives. We served in a host of roles through ten different senior pastors and at three different sanctuaries (two now razed, with new college buildings on top of them). Wilda became a fixture as Sunday school secretary, teacher, and missionary leader. I served as church organist, children's choir director, bell choir director, instrumental music director, and more.

Our roles have diminished, though I still play the organ for the Sunday evening service. College Wesleyan Church is all that my wife and I really know, and we continue to consider ourselves available for God's service. Amid all of the blessings I've noted, we still have some unfulfilled dreams of anticipated blessings for College Wesleyan Church. God, of course, is able to fulfill them at his discretion.

Each Sunday as we step into the sanctuary, we praise God for the longevity of strong leadership that decided to design a sacred space. Instead of a utilitarian multipurpose room, we enter a sanctuary that has a fifty-foot-high point and strategic stained-glass windows that teach prominent Bible lessons; and a platform surrounded by marble large enough to hold orchestras, bell choirs, drama teams, and other traditional expressions—in addition to many modern ones. The Communion table is still there, along with the altar rails—all made from wood reclaimed from our former church building.

I may be in the sunset years, and at times I'm keenly aware that the majority of members have preferences different than mine, but we share in common the sacred space, and the sacred truths on which it was built.

NOTE

1. Bob Dylan, "*The Times They Are A-Changin'*," recorded 1963, 1964, Warner Bros. Inc., renewed 1991, 1992, Special Rider Music.

A FORMER WORLD LEADER MAY BE IN THE NEXT PEW

EVELYN BENCE

Editor's Note: *Sometimes rock stars in many locations go relatively unnoticed in others, even in their own churches. Christian leaders on the world stage usually have their own home churches and, like Dr. Robert Lytle, may slip into services unrecognized by most fellow members. Dr. Lytle died in 2011 at ninety-three years old, several years after the death of his wife, Louise, who had shared his illustrious career as pastor, missionary, and general secretary (director) of Wesleyan World Missions. While a hero and lifelong role model to thousands, he could sing choruses next to hundreds who weren't born until after his retirement in 1984.*

A notion often shared from pulpits is that the gospel story is perpetually one generation from extinction. Although this isn't in sync with scriptural promises or Old Testament accounts of Moses' law being lost for generations, it resonates with the role we play in keeping it alive for the next generation. For the villages and cities that Dr. Lytle touched either through his own service or the missionaries he mentored, the gospel will indeed remain vibrant, at least into the next generation. This account is written by a respected writer and editor, whose brother, Bud Bence, has also spent decades as a member at College Wesleyan Church, sometimes sitting alongside his uncle, Bob Lytle.

▼ ▼ ▼

"Great is thy faithfulness!" Bob Lytle, veteran missionary, heartily sang this hymn as his life theme.

Bob recalled the day when Thomas Chisholm's hymn, inspired by pivotal lines of Jeremiah's Lamentations, was indelibly stamped on his consciousness. It was 1945, the year he, his wife, Louise, and their infant son, left New York for their first missionary tour.

The Lytles flew to Colombia, but they couldn't board the plane with much baggage, being restricted to sixty pounds for each paying passenger. And most of that allotment, Bob said, "was claimed by diapers and baby necessities. Mom and Pop had little room for their clothing and household articles"—including many items unavailable in the Third World. With the exception of bare essentials, Bob and Louise had packed everything to be shipped by sea. They were told to expect the boxes and barrels to arrive at their door in three weeks.

In Medellin, the Lytles moved into a mission apartment outfitted with basic furnishings. But weeks, then months, passed, and Bob started to wonder if the boat had sailed to Calcutta. "Our son lived comfortably with plenty of diapers and rompers. But the parents—we watched our insufficient clothing become damaged, worn out, and detested. We longed for the 'useful gadgets' packed away and gone only God knew where," he said.

Bob and Louise prayed for God's merciful will, and finally six months later, the unaccompanied baggage arrived on two rickety, two-wheeled, horse-drawn flatbeds. Though battered, it had survived its sea voyage, the sunbaked docks, the customs inspection, and the train trip up the Andes from the coast.

The morning those tired horses stopped in the street, he said, "it happened—no, God ruled it—that a fellow missionary in a neighboring apartment was playing 'Great Is Thy Faithfulness' on her vibraharp." Bob remembered the moment: "My spirit rose with that song as I thought how good, how faithful, God had been. In hindsight, I see that the cartons may have contained only a few trinkets, but he had brought them in blessing to us."

Bob saw God's faithfulness not only in providing the long-delayed possessions, but also in the timing of a neighbor's song of praise. "It was more than a fortuitous happening," he said about the music vibrating through the thin walls. It was God's not-so-subtle reminder—strong enough to last a lifetime—that he is Jehovah-jireh, the God who sees and the God whose provision shall be seen. That event was followed by uncounted encores, daily blessings, small and large, that reinforced this lesson learned as a young man.

And yet there would be days when Bob could have written his own litany of lamentations. And that's when he chose to take Jeremiah's tack—relying on recollection of previously acquired knowledge and understanding: "This I recall to mind, therefore I have hope" (Lam. 3:21 KJV).

As we face a new morning, let us remember to recount God's faithfulness. Recollect his mercies. Recall the small and large miracles of our lives. The material provisions. The orchestrated interventions. The reasons for our hope.[1]

This I recall to my mind, therefore have I hope. It is of the LORD's
mercies that we are not consumed, because his compassions fail not.
They are new every morning: great is thy faithfulness.
—Lamentations 3:21–23 (KJV)

NOTE

1. Adapted from Evelyn Bence, *Spiritual Moments with the Great Hymns* (Grand Rapids, MI : Zondervan, 1997). Used by permission of the author.

PART 2

THE **TRUTH**
OF **GOD'S**
COMFORT

AFTER A CADILLAC,
WHY SETTLE FOR A CHEVY?

BEVERLEY BAILEY

Editor's Note: *When all the cake is served and the coffee runs low, funeral logistics begin to register with the grieving host. The throng of friends, all well-meaning, will leave the widow or widower alone. The last guest leaves with the most generous expressions of love. Many friends have offered help, often at sacrificial levels. Various genuine expressions speak volumes of their depth of love and appreciation for both the departed and the griever. But as the hours pass, the reality sets in: at some point in the evening the house will be eerily quiet. Although I married Cindy when she was a young widow and realize that this scenario plays out in homes worldwide, I'm also struck by how unique each situation is. There are common steps, familiar grieving stages, and frequent missteps that become funny in retrospect, but the lost life brings unique survival stories. Getting on with life takes such different directions for each survivor. And sometimes the choices could not be more different between the survivors. In the following pages, we are treated to the personal journal from the days surrounding Beverley's loss at a young age. We also catch a glimpse of a journey all too familiar to many readers even as we get better acquainted with a spunky and invigorating woman. I first read this story while sitting at the Congregation House at University Church, a café next to Oxford's Radcliffe Camera. I turned to a professor-friend, who* *was sharing the table and asked if I could read aloud this touching story. I assume you'll pass along this chapter as well.*

▼   ▼   ▼

Words were unnecessary. My friend's eyes said it all, and I instinctively backed away from him—sensing fear. I wanted to run, to remove myself from his eyes, but he caught me. He ignored my words as I begged, "Just tell me he isn't dead." My friend wouldn't speak—yet his eyes held the truth. He wrapped his arms around me and held on. No reassuring words, just silence. I collapsed onto the driveway—a memory forever frozen.

Life as I knew it came to a screeching halt on June 7, 1995. That's the day I learned my husband had suffered an aortic aneurysm. In a heartbeat, half of me was viciously ripped away without warning. The hurt was deep and agonizing. It hurt midday, in the middle of the night, and in the center of my stomach.

I silently screamed questions and declarations: "He's too young to die! I'm too young to be a widow! We're only forty-eight. How can I possibly go on when half of me is gone?"

We had been soul mates since we were twelve years old. When he inhaled, I exhaled. God gave us the gift for thirty-six years—twenty-nine of them in marriage. "Lord, I've already lost a child, and now this?" Cards poured in; so many comforting, loving words. Some from people I barely knew; others from people I had never met. They explained how Willis had touched their lives and expressed soothing and healing sentiments. Perhaps I shouldn't admit this, but those who quoted or wrote Scripture seemed the least comforting. I didn't need platitudes, reasons, or explanations about God's will. All I wanted to hear was that you were hurting too. The truth is, I just needed people to help me cry.

The following are eight journal entries intended to capture both the events and the lessons of that season. I share them, hoping that others might find them helpful in their own journey or as they walk alongside others who grieve.

Sunday, June 4: God gave us a beautiful gift. The sermon theme was on marriage and we had prepared the perfect song. We stood looking into each other's eyes as we sang, "I Cherish the Treasure," by Jon Mohr: "Lifelong companion. I give myself to you."[1]

Monday, June 5: I went to the office and sneaked up behind Willis, slipping my arm into his. "You wanna go for our last lunch?" I asked. Just a silly question since I was leaving town for a few days— but so prophetic. We had a delightful time talking and planning, and then we parted and he went back to the office.

The ladies and I met at 3:30 and stood in a circle while he prayed for safe travel and our planning retreat. I gave him a hug and kiss, said, "I love you," and we headed for Wisconsin to a lake house belonging to Paul and Val. That's the last time I saw him alive.

Tuesday, June 6: Willis called in sick. He even made an appointment to see the doctor at 2 p.m. Strange, what man does that? Nothing appeared to be serious . . . probably just the flu. He picked up a few things at the grocery and went home to bed. At approximately 10:00 p.m. his thoracic aorta burst . . . three to five heartbeats, and he was gone. No pain or suffering, he just peacefully slipped off to heaven—no one knowing until the next day.

Wednesday, June 7: Marti led our morning prayer time and she asked each of the ladies to pray aloud for *me*—particularly for that day. Strange, but sweet. "Who doesn't need prayer?" I thought. Only God knew who would be in distress, and Marti's heart listened to his prompting.

When Willis didn't go to or call the office, three messages were left on our answering machine and no calls returned. After lunch they decided to check on him. Finley rang the bell, knocked, and walked around the house pounding on all the windows. No response except from the dog. Seriously concerned, he called Brian—a police officer from our congregation, and they managed to get in through the sliding glass door. They found him in bed with our little dog, Mozart, standing guard. He was gone. It was 1:45 p.m.

We left Wisconsin at 1:50 p.m. Paul called the lake house, but we were already out the door. His wife, Val, the only person with a cell phone, had neglected to turn it on. What a blessing. (It was unusual to have a cell phone in 1995, and they were used only for emergencies.) We were able to have a carefree, fun trip home.

We stopped for gas and a friend from church was at the traffic light; she began yelling to Val, "Have you been home?" Val answered no, and the woman shouted, "Go home now!" The urgency in her voice caused Val to jump quickly back into the van and race the few blocks to her house. We prayed all the way for what might be awaiting her.

When we drove up, Paul entered the house from the garage, and Val ran inside. I could see her kids in the kitchen. Everything seemed to be in order. We breathed a sigh of relief, got out of the car, and waited in the drive. Then Paul and Val came out, and he started walking toward me. His eyes locked on mine and I knew.

It was bad and it belonged to me!

Thursday, June 8: I insisted on seeing him. He lay on a gurney covered with a sheet. When I recovered from the shock of his lifeless body, I leaned in close and gently tapped my fingers against his cheek. "Wake up," I whispered over and over. He didn't stir. I've never felt so utterly alone or exposed. It was like a dull knife slowly cutting through my heart.

Friday, June 10: Our anniversary was far from my mind as I went through the motions of greeting people at calling hours. Some people say the dumbest things! When I stepped aside for water, I told Pastor Dan, "If I haul off and hit someone, just tell them I'm grieving and can't be held responsible for my actions!" He just grinned and gave me a bear hug.

Sunday, June 11: We chose to have a celebration service in the evening. It seemed so fitting for Willis. He would have loved the music, the eulogy, the memories shared by friends. . . . I felt his final approval!

Monday, June 12: The morning interment. This whole process took seven days! Mourning is anything but comfortable.

Sunday night I experienced an incredible intimacy. I was trying to fall asleep, but my shoulders felt so cold. The memory of falling asleep with the warmth of his arm draped over my shoulder overwhelmed me. As I cried, I felt the tender warmth of an arm move across my back and shoulder giving me a gentle squeeze. Suddenly all of my senses were on overload! I was in awe and didn't want the feeling to fade. I lay there relaxing in the warmth and presence of that arm until I finally drifted off to sleep . . . secure in God's unfailing arms. That moment has never left my memory. Truly God is a husband to the widow (see Isa. 54:5).

Mother said I'll make it because I've never been a crybaby. She reminded me that when I was five years old a friend fell off his bike and went home screaming to his mama. I came in the house, looked out the window, and said, "Look at that great big kid cryin' like that!"

"You never had time for pity," she continued. "You've always picked yourself up and started again." Well, this was a little different. This hurt deserved a little time for pity. But eventually I'd have to pick myself up and keep going. Was there another choice?

Why haven't I remarried? It's simple: God hasn't provided the right man! A friend asked, "After you've had a Cadillac, how will you settle for a Chevy?"

"I won't," I answered. "I'll get another Cadillac!"

Now, twenty years later, God still hasn't provided the Cadillac, but I'm good. I'm really good! He has faithfully redeemed my pain and transformed my life; and he continues to create in me a new person, molding me into his image. My life is what I am given *now*.

I don't know how my story will end, but nowhere in the text will it ever read: she went home cryin'.

NOTE

1. Jon Mohr, *"I Cherish the Treasure,"* recorded 1988, Birdwing Music.

OUR BOYS SLEPT WHILE I WEPT
WIDOWED ON FATHER'S DAY EVE

CINDY PATTENGALE

Editor's Note: *This story is especially dear to me, as I've been the father of the boys mentioned below for the past twenty-five years. The story of Cindy's loss was familiar because it played on the news throughout the country. I was living in Glendora, California, in a two-room cabin in the San Bernardino Mountains, not far from Azusa Pacific University where I taught. Life was busy and blissful, though I longed for a Christian wife and eventually a family. Little did I know what God had in store for the near future. Through mutual friends, I met Cindy. I had known hardship. I had experienced change. But Cindy's change was brutally abrupt. It's a story of successful survival, of God's grace and provisions. I can attest to her godly character and daily routines, as God must smile as he watches and walks with her. She never tries to impress him, only to please him.*

▼ ▼ ▼

When I told our boys on Father's Day morning in 1989 that their young father had died, the holiday was over.

The boys were asleep when I returned from the hospital, numb and exhausted. In the morning when I awoke, it seemed like a dream. Oh, I hoped it was. On a day intended to celebrate their energetic dad, I had to inform my boys they no longer had him. Jason was six, the eldest. I awoke him first. Josh was three and simply didn't understand. Nick was just eleven months old. I could only hold him, knowing that in the decades ahead he'd realize that the brutal event of the night before had changed his life.

The evening at the waterfront was perfect at first as David and I joined my parents and siblings for a boat ride before supper. We ate at Shooters Restaurant at Portside, on the banks of the Maumee River in downtown Toledo, Ohio.

When it looked like rain might fall, my dad went to move his fifty-foot boat a bit closer. David and I strolled to the indicated dock. While waiting for the boat, we enjoyed a quiet moment, hugging and saying we loved each other. But then three small speedboats pulled up, carrying teenage boys. When we asked them to wait so my parents' boat could fit in too, they ignored us. After everyone docked, I walked back to the restaurant, thinking David followed right behind me. But then I saw a crowd by the restaurant gathering and pointing at the dock. When I turned back around toward the boat and found my mom, she wouldn't let me get on the dock.

"Honey, I love you." David's last words to me on what had been a relaxing, overcast sunset on the water, seared themselves into my mind. Moments later his life was snuffed out. As he turned the corner to follow me, he glanced back and was startled by the sight of a speedboat driver—upset over the parking space reserved for larger boats—pummeling his father-in-law on the peer.

Then, unseen and unexpected, a large seventeen-year-old, one of the speedboat passengers, punched David in the back of the head. The crushing blow from the local football player knocked my vibrant, healthy husband into a diving platform. Rendered unconscious, David fell into the water and slipped out of sight beneath the dock.

Both my brother and dad jumped in to rescue him. The next few nightmarish minutes are never discussed. All their energy, emotion, and exhausted efforts proved futile. Emergency divers answering a 911 call heroically retrieved David and rushed him to the hospital. We followed, thinking they had saved him.

I remember, in the waiting room, praying over and over that David would be OK, anticipating that he would be alright. Life with David had never been dull; he had a knack for getting hurt. Our first year of marriage, he'd been robbed and stabbed, and then a month later at work, as a carpenter, he'd cut three fingers on a circular saw. The list was long. I thought I was ready to add another crisis.

After about twenty minutes of this, sensing that God knew all things, I felt that I should ask God to do what was best for David. This was an unusual prayer for me; I don't really know where it came from. Around five minutes later, the doctor soberly informed us that David hadn't made it.

What? I was too young to be a widow. We had three small sons. David was young and healthy! How could this be? I went in to see him, and indeed his body lay lifeless. The contagious smile was gone, his blue eyes shut. He was now with the Lord.

A teenager's tragic, senseless, foolish swing took a life that had exploded with energy. All these years later, tears still form amidst the laughter when friends reminisce, mimic his mannerisms, or recall his relentless humor.

The football player was found guilty of involuntary manslaughter but, because he was a minor, he received the legal sentence of five weekends in detention. Some friends convinced me, for our sons' sake, to file a civil claim, but I eventually dropped the lawsuit after technicalities delayed decisions and thus prolonged agonizing reflections. Also, I felt God wanted me to show mercy toward the other family, considering their pain for their son.

Life pushed ahead and a couple of years later Jerry and I married. My sons accepted him into their lives. When thieves stole the moving truck and trailer a week after our honeymoon (near Christmas), a few hand tools stored in Toledo were all that remained from David's earthly "treasures." That is, all but his wonderful reputation.

Later, our oldest son, Jason, showed me the carpenter tools he and Papa had retrieved from storage and restored. I can only imagine what went through Jason's mind when he held his dad's hammer for the first time and when he cleaned the wrenches and repainted the toolbox. Today, Jason is in his early thirties and lives with his wife in Anchorage, Alaska. Perhaps it's fitting that he's a carpenter.

I value a recent letter from an old friend of David's. Around the time of Jason's birth, David had remodeled a room for this friend, who'd paid him by check. Not wanting to lose the check, David had tacked it to a stud. But then he inadvertently finished the wall with the check still inside. Lost to the ages.

The letter, addressed to Jason, recounted the story. The family was remodeling again. Tearing out the wall, they'd found the check still nailed to the stud. David's friend enclosed the check, now among Jason's prized possessions. He'll hold on to it tightly, along with the hammer.

Jason also holds fast to positive memories. True character stands the test of time. For Jason and his biological brothers, Nick and Josh, the image of their father is frozen—and through the years friends and relatives have helped to add resolution to the picture.

All fathers face moments when they recognize the fleeting passage of life. What few things will their children grasp, hold tightly? And what image will be frozen in their memories? I'm regularly reminded of such questions, especially around Father's Day.

I have learned that the frozen image represents a sum of memories; children know our character and characteristics well. Each day we're being mentally filmed. In the end, it's usually not how parents died, but how we lived, that remains central to our legacy.

In one of Jerry's books, he included the following dedication that captured the grandeur of David's large and magnetic personality:

> To the memory of David E. Tiller (1957–1989)
> He was full of life and lives on in Jason, Joshua, and Nicholas,
> my three eldest sons. I have not met a person from his life who
> doesn't miss him, and I look forward to the introductions
> in heaven—where his smile will last forever.

I have sensed a sad reality of David's loss: that he was the very person who would have been the best help through the pain, the countless nights of tears, and long stretches of loneliness. Some of you reading this can empathize, perhaps having lost precious friends or family, a child, or a spouse. I realize that this is a dark journey of the soul. Some experiences or seasons cannot be painted completely in pastels. There's nothing pretty about sin. Nothing to celebrate. No prompting of rejoicing when you're shocked into the reality of such a senseless loss. But I'd be remiss not to share a few lessons. I'm not an educator. But I think God has, in his special way, helped me to understand this life a bit better—and with an eternal perspective.

I know that God provides. It's one of his names, Jehovah-jireh. Many people brought food and money after my husband's passing. David and I had taken out life insurance only two years prior. We got Social Security money which allowed me to stay home with the children even after moving to California after remarriage. And, somehow, we managed to put our boys, including our fourth son, through private education for most of the K–12 and college years.

God helped me to increase spiritually, growth that previously had been, at best, a seed. God met me. As I walked, I felt his hand in mine. As a relatively new believer, saved along with David when Jason was one year old, I trusted God. Like a baby, I reached out with simple but sincere faith. Oh, I cried and got frustrated. I grieved till I ached. But at each juncture, he was right beside me, giving me strength to continue.

I learned to cherish prayer. When I prayed at the beginning of this journey, I felt the prayers of others holding me up. And I also felt when those prayers waned. This was my biggest area of growth. I was learning to pray more often, not long periods of intercession but short, constant prayer.

Basically, I learned to trust God in hard times—some of the toughest of times were when two of our older sons fought chronic diseases; cancer and Crohn's. God has been my provider many times in tangible and intangible ways. God manifests himself in infinite ways. Through this life journey, he's helping me to see these manifestations with a sustaining clarity.

HIDDEN TREASURES
IN THE DARKNESS

JACKIE WHITE

Editor's Note: Some people only see the glass half empty; then others, like Jackie, see it not only half full but can envision the other half also full and overflowing. Oh, she's a realist, able to size up situations and give politely candid appraisals, but she's got that scarlet "G" on her sweater for "genuine."

Years ago my wife, Cindy, accepted a part-time role in our church office, more to help the ministry and be with the staff than for a job. It wasn't long before she came home bubbling over, often sharing such funny exchanges with Jackie, who would soon become one of her good friends and, in time, one of mine. I had played tennis with her brother, Steve, in college but never imagined he'd become the "Rev. DeNeff" who would pastor the church I attended. Or that his sister would become such a vital part of our place of worship and our lives.

There are people you meet in life who you realize would crawl across the Sahara if that were needed to help a person and nobody else was available. That's Jackie. And perhaps there's no more fulfilling email to receive than when she writes, truly tickled by something I've written, or blessed by it (or carefully disagreeing). This has been the routine for this book, as she has been the point person. Ironically, it took coaching to have her submit her own story—which was vetted like the rest. It's here because it speaks with an uncanny sensitivity about the journey from the wedding altar to the grave when disease eclipses romance for a season. But it's only for a little while.

I'm reminded when reading her story of the pain and promise of my days researching in Baltimore at the Johns Hopkins History of Medicine Center. As I entered the back of the hospital from Rose Hall, I was actually entering through the original front of the grand hospital—now repurposed and mainly used by interns. But every dawn began a new day and challenge. And there, in the grand old entrance, stood a ten-foot statue of Jesus with his arms stretched wide. He dominated the rotunda. I would read these words which are engraved on the pedestal: "Come unto me, all ye that are weary and heavy laden and I will give you rest (Matt. 11:28)." And, as Jackie hints below, each dawn those same arms carry her through and help her to embrace hope and find joy. Each dawn is a divine promise.

▼ ▼ ▼

Someone once said that when you stand at the altar and promise before family and friends "to love, honor, and cherish; through sickness and in health, until death parts you," you're thinking of the flu, not an extended disease like dementia. I don't recall even thinking about the flu; I was so elated to be getting married—finally.

My wedding plans began when I was only twelve. But decades later came a memorable night when I looked across the room and found only a faint reminder of the man with whom I had exchanged vows. So much of him had been swallowed up in the cavernous abyss of his dementia, an ugly illness. It consumed most of my recent years. For most of my life, I've believed that God does not call us to anything we cannot do. Without him, perhaps we couldn't; but with him, we can. On that memorable night, however, I collapsed in my reflections: "But this is hard! I am tired."

That night will stay with me through many seasons. I recall thinking, "My heart is exhausted by all the losses; so many of them unexpected. Yet with today's loss, another piece of me has fallen into this black hole of no return. Part of me wonders if I'll ever get it back, and the other part wonders if I would have the energy for it if I did get it back. Today I am in limbo, somewhere between real life and the grand exit to another." Perhaps you might find this odd, but my thoughts came to an unexpected realization: "I've found a respite in limbo. Here I can cope, doing the next manual task, as if I'm on autopilot."

I had watched *The Notebook* a few weeks before the above night. It's a 2004 drama film that totally romanticizes the life of a woman with Alzheimer's. Her devoted husband visits daily and reads to her the story of their life together. Throughout the drama, James Garner narrates and the lead actors, Ryan Gosling and Rachel McAdams, envelop the story in enchanted believability. At the close of the movie, they end up peacefully dying together in the same twin bed, arm in arm, as if wishing it so could possibly make it happen. All neat, tidy, without messes. On that memorable night I cried, "Oh, I long, I hurt for such an ending to my saga."

A debilitating mind and body is not easily romanticized. The heart is wrecked by the uncertainty that lies waiting with each new dawn. Life is messy and unpredictable.

I've learned that the promise makes it all possible.

After getting my husband showered and dressed for the second time one day, I left for Walmart to do the unthinkable. How on earth do you buy diapers for your husband of twenty-three years? I cannot begin to express the level of grief that overwhelmed me. Such incredible loss! My mind processed many silent questions. Is this what it feels like when your lover dies? It was as if someone had sucked all the air out of the world and I was left gasping.

This is the worst loss yet, I thought. As I carried the package in, my husband looked at me with some of the most disappointed eyes I've ever seen. As I bent over to put the underwear on him, he quietly said, "Really?"

"It'll be fine," I said, trying to reassure him. "No one will even know you have them on. They'll be under your pants." And that was the end of it. No argument. No fuss. Wow! Even in this, God was teaching me something. In that moment, I saw what it meant to be grace filled in the midst of adversity. I thought, "Lord, help me to be compliant when I need to be. Help me to make it easy for others to care for me when it's my time."

Sometime in the middle of the night, great sorrow awakened me. *I can't make it through this anymore.* God asked me to get up and read. *I can't. I'm too tired.* He quietly reminded me of his past promises. And I knew it was true, that whenever God bids me come near, he fills my heart with his words. Imperishable and tried. Tested through the fire and now gold. So I pulled myself out of bed, tiptoed into the sitting room, and turned to the passage to which he led me: Isaiah 45:2–4 (NLT). As I began reading, I was unable to hold back the tears.

This is what the LORD says: "I will go before you, Cyrus, and level the mountains. I will smash down gates of bronze and cut through bars of iron. And I will give you treasures hidden in the darkness— secret riches. I will do this so you may know that I am the LORD, the God of Israel, the one who calls you by name. And why have I called you for this work? Why did I call you by name when you did not know me? It is for the sake of Jacob my servant, Israel my chosen one."

My heart grew quiet and pondered God's goodness. I knew I was not alone in this endeavor, that there were good things in all of this. I simply needed to look for them. I left the room that night with a different perspective. Yes, life is hard; there's no doubt about it. But I am not alone. In those treasures, hidden in this darkness, I will find joy.

My husband would live two and a half more years after that memorable night. But as the Lord promised, every day thereafter, came a moment that was unmistakably, irrefutably divine. A moment when God whispered, "I love you. You are mine. This moment is your treasure, tucked away in this darkness."

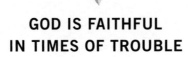

GOD IS FAITHFUL
IN TIMES OF TROUBLE

TERESA FRANCIS

Editor's Note: *For the past twenty years, about every time Teresa parted our company, I'd comment to my wife, "She is such a special woman." That is, if Cindy didn't beat me to the punch. Until reading this story, I had never heard her talk about the tough routine, indeed a daily grind of absolute necessity, she undertook to help sustain her husband's life and her family's livelihood. Our kids went to church with hers, and her son attended their school. We saw her often, which only accentuated our admiration. And atop her marathon care for her increasingly disabled husband, she was the most reliable of youth sponsors at church. Not just being present, but acting as the long-established planner. She became the fulcrum of activities for the substantial JCBodyshop student ministries.*

One day she hosted a party at her home, a modest but nice house tucked away in a thick and largely uncontrollable woods. I suddenly realized that the inner strength of this woman was like a special metal, and to mix the metaphor, titanium tough. She was caring for a demanding property that her husband had once managed, for kids her husband had once helped raise, and for bills resourced by no second income. She had windows to fix, weeds to whack, a sidewalk to fix, and trees to trim—all on top of a grueling routine of caring for her husband and kids. I'm convinced that few men will ever die with more assurance of a wife's undying love, and few spouses will ever have ministered to more people unintentionally while very intentionally fulfilling their marriage vows.

▼ ▼ ▼

Isaiah 43:2–3 (ESV) says, "When you pass through the waters, I will be with you; and through the rivers, they shall not overwhelm you. . . . For I am the LORD your God." When my husband was diagnosed with Huntington's disease, I had to depend on God to be with me and our young children.

Huntington's disease is a neurological disorder that causes the progressive breakdown of nerve cells in the brain; it has a broad debilitating impact on motor, cognitive, and psychiatric faculties.

As we prayed for healing for Gary, his symptoms grew worse. In a sermon during this troubling progression, a pastor said that it is always within God's power to heal the sick, but it is not always in his plan. Through these perplexing days, I often referred to Jeremiah 29:11 (ESV): "'For I know the plans I have for you' declares the LORD, 'plans . . . to give you a future and a hope.'" As Gary's disease progressed, he had to give up his work, and eventually he couldn't drive. These and other traumatic transitions prompted depression, mood swings, and paranoia that worried and taxed all of us. Gary's radical changes confused our children and saddened me deeply. What had happened to our idyllic family life together?

God's grace and mercy continued, nevertheless. Gary's loss of income forced me to find a way to provide for our family and our church day care offered me a job teaching preschool. At the time, I questioned why I didn't get a public school position to earn more money, but God's perfect timing, and blessing, became evident: I could take our four-year-old son and third-grade daughter with me to work when Gary was no longer able to care for them alone.

Two years later, God was still leading in our lives. I received a phone inquiry during the summer from a special-needs director in the Mississinewa Community Schools system. The next day I interviewed, and the following day I was hired to teach a preschool special-needs class. I hadn't even applied for the job, but God orchestrated a perfect fit. After two years in that position, I moved into a kindergarten grade level, where I've now taught for twenty years.

Eventually Gary's condition spiraled downward; his living at home was no longer safe for him or for us. I still loved this dear man, although, through his diction and demeanor, his actions and reactions—faculties beyond his control—he seemed like a stranger to me.

I made the hardest decision of my life: to place him in a nursing home. I had married him "for better or for worse," and this was definitely "for worse."

As I contacted several care facilities, God's plan once again became evident. The one that was able to admit him was in Gas City, where I was teaching. A couple of years later, my school was closed, and I was transferred to the other local school—right beside the nursing home! I had already been visiting him every day; now I was able to run over during my lunch break if our children had activities after school that kept me away.

Gary's disease continued to progress. Soon he couldn't walk, talk, or feed himself. The last few days of his life, we were blessed to have all of our extended family gather in, by his bedside. Through many tears, we reminisced about our good memories with Gary.

The day Gary passed from this life to his heavenly home, visitors who prayed for Gary and for our family heartened us. With permission, an Indiana Wesleyan University professor whom we knew brought a crisis management class. The concern and prayers of these strangers—evidence of God's love—made a huge impact on Gary's family.

Through this arduous journey, God proved faithful to his promises to be with us. We had wonderful support from our families and an amazing church family. I reckon you're not surprised that one of my favorite songs is "Great Is Thy Faithfulness." He truly provides strength for each day, no matter its gravity or levity. And in this season of life, I'm glad there's a bit more of the latter.

PART 3

THE TRUTH OF GOD'S GRACE

CARRYING ELIJAH
THE TRANSFORMATIVE JOURNEY OF LOVING AND LOSING MY CHILD

BRITTANI SCHMIDT

Editor's Note: *Sometimes seventy-three minutes seems like a lifetime. In the story below, it was. Brittani shares what could have been simply a gut-wrenching summary of the loss of a newborn son. Instead, she celebrates his brief life. But there's another dynamic at play in this story—our being able to empathize with fellow church members. At least three church families have had similar infant fatalities within the past few years. All of the couples determined to carry the baby full term, even against medical warnings and advice on abortion. All the babies were diagnosed with kidney issues, coupled with other complications. And all shared brief moments on this earth before tasting heaven.*

I know such heartache too well, because our oldest son and his wife experienced the loss of their daughter in similar circumstances. The timing of Brittani's chapter surfaced in my editing queue at perhaps the worst time. It was the very day our kids went to the funeral home to prepare for their own daughter's passing. Trite statements abound at times like this, and most of us really don't know how best to support those enduring such tragedies. When I finally was less emotional and returned weeks later to edit this story, I could see it in a new light. In our church, there are others who have endured this sorrow. In the broader church, many resources from a host of experiences articulate steps to restoration. Perhaps the story below won't ease anyone's pain or be easy reading for those who aren't close to such situations. But part of membership in a church community is becoming familiar with fellow congregants' journeys and welcoming their transparency. And a key aspect of entering into such tragic stories is coming to a fuller realization of how God assists and blesses others in their struggles.

▼   ▼   ▼

A few years ago, my world turned upside down. What should have been a joyful time was far from it. My husband and I were expecting our third child with bated breath. We were going to have three small children under the age of five. For the most part, life was bliss and getting better.

We suppose most couples fear one of those alarming phone calls about an endangered child or the doctor sitting them down for a talk of tragic proportions. Such a moment came for us when I was at eighteen weeks' gestation. Highly abnormal test results indicated a problem with our baby. Thanksgiving of 2011 was only two days away, and we found ourselves at St. Vincent's Hospital in Indianapolis. The specialized ultrasound produced results that stopped our world. We suspected Down Syndrome based on previous consultations with doctors, but the scan revealed a much worse diagnosis. Our son did not develop kidneys. He would not be able to live outside my womb. Nearly paralyzing grief overtook us.

The journey of carrying my son Elijah lasted another fourteen weeks and during this time God showed up—in big and small ways, in everyday activities, and in the love of his people.

From the very day of that fateful diagnosis, the Lord and his church surrounded and carried us. Some days getting out of bed seemed an insurmountable feat. Some days the tears hardly stopped flowing. But the magnitude of our pain was met with intense love and acts of kindness.

A dear friend, who at the time was more of an acquaintance, brought us dinner every Monday. She wanted a tangible weekly reminder to pray for us and love on us. Friends, family, and church members called often. Many sent flowers, prayed for us "without ceasing," and watched our children on short notice. They allowed us to have some times alone to process our situation, basically, to survive. Their actions regularly reminded us that we were not alone.

Though the time was heartbreaking, I am so thankful for it. I would never trade away the months, the moments, I carried Elijah. I would have missed the palpable presence of God that covered us. I would never trade who I am now for who I was before.

The ripple effect from Elijah's abbreviated life continues to amaze me. We never could have anticipated the depth of learning and range of blessings that followed. By fully trusting God, we hopefully allowed his work to be done. Perhaps the following excerpt from my blog captures a portion of the intense change in our lives from these few months. We continue to experience growth; our lives' changes are certainly still in motion.

November 30, 2011: It's been interesting to ride the wave of emotions we navigated last week. Some of them I expected, some I never saw coming. The most unusual thing I've experienced this week is something I couldn't even grasp, because it didn't seem to fit. I had to grapple with it for a couple of days before even mentioning it to Kyle. When I mentioned it to my small group tonight, I found myself trying to wade through it; it didn't seem to come out right. But, oddly enough, I feel excitement. Please don't get me wrong . . . there is nothing exciting about what we are going through. I don't get excited when I break down in my husband's or my best friend's arms. I don't get excited when my kids see me weeping and sweetly try to comfort me. There is nothing exciting about looking through sewing patterns of outfits to choose the one I will eventually bury my child in. The only thing that I know is exciting is that God always works for good in the lives of his people . . . and I know that he is going to use this situation . . . our lives, our baby's life . . . some aspect of our earthly nightmare to further his kingdom. We may never know what impact this little life will have on others, but God knows. We are told in Scripture that the Lord knows all our days, before there are any. That means that while we were blindsided by this situation, he wasn't. He knew what we would endure before we were even born. He has a plan, and only he can give this sense of peace, comfort, and, oddly enough, excitement, in a season of uncertainty and pain.[1]

All praise to the One who is able to do this!

Elijah's earthly journey ended in the early hours of a blustery Leap Day morning. In that quiet hospital room, with my husband and best friend, Elijah was intensely loved in his seventy-three minutes with us. He was dedicated over the phone by Pastor Steve DeNeff, and in person by Pastor Judy Crossman. We would later learn that at the same moment Elijah left us, Pastor Steve was prompted to again consecrate our baby to the Lord. What a beautiful welcome home he must have received!

I sit now, rocking my six-month-old daughter, a surprise blessing from God. I listen to her tiny breaths and thank God daily for his continued faithfulness in all the seen and unseen moments of my life. I praise him for never leaving my side, in the sorrow and in the joy. I praise him for real, authentic friends who so beautifully "do life" with us at College Wesleyan Church. And I praise him for his relentless love, a small taste of which I get to lavish on my children, the ones I can hold in my arms here, and my Elijah, whom I will always hold in my heart.

NOTE

1. Brittani Schmidt, brittschmidt.blogspot.com.

RAPED BUT NOT RUINED

RACHEL HENRY

Editor's Note: *A single event can storm a community, paralyzing some sectors and infuriating others. The narrative below is such a story. It's also one of God's faithfulness and an outpouring of love demonstrated in such a pronounced way. As this goes to press, two of the three young men are beginning forty-year prison terms, with emphasis on young (all were teens at the time of the event). The third pleaded guilty and is awaiting his sentence.*

*When the victim, Rachel, submitted this piece for the book, my heart dropped. Suddenly I was being asked to help the world to hear her side, to help capture the pain, lessons, and then the joy of God's provisions. I've done my best, but it's really one of those stories where God needs to do the rest. Rachel and Simon are the type of couple you'd find in Sunday school promotions—*GQ *handsome and* Vogue *beautiful, with children reminiscent of adorable kids' ads—including magnetic twins. Simon was among my best students and served as my assistant for two years. Rachel is sister to another striking individual, our daughter-in-law. In the immediate aftermath of this crime, her godly heartbroken parents stayed with us. Like much of the city, and readers nationally, their plight seemed to be ours. We searched for answers, justice, and healing. The episode below played out in much detail in local and national papers. Now it's Rachel's turn to speak.*

▼ ▼ ▼

When three hooded invaders threatened to kill our four children, my body became the only door to their survival. That horrid option became a decision I'll never regret, or forget. I was left with no option and a vivid memory that will never entirely fade. Every one of our kids' smiles, tears, joys, and fears is a precious reminder of God's sustaining love. They are alive.

In some ways that dark night is a blur. In others, it's as if someone reached out and stopped the earth's rotation on its axis, and time itself.

The irony of the incident is that my husband is rarely away from home at nights. But on this fateful July day in 2014, he was and, perhaps accenting the uneven fate, only a few blocks away. Simon was fulfilling a residency requirement for his doctoral program at the college where he also works. The campus lies just past the stalwart church where we worship. The double irony is that within a stone's throw from the horrific attack was our spiritual retreat, our refuge, our crossroads with some of the best Christian friends we could hope for. And a few steps farther is one of the nation's largest Christian campuses, where I learned of a powerful God, a faithful Friend, and an omniscient, just Creator. But on this night, it's what those institutions helped ingrain within me that made the difference, not whether I could find refuge within their walls. I couldn't reach my own door, let alone their environs.

Amidst the ordeal, a peace prevailed; God could hug me through and beyond the harsh embraces of these juvenile rapists. There would be life beyond this. Our kids would live beyond the night as well.

Our little house was on a busy street, and intruders would have had to be the most aggressive and fearless—and that's exactly what I confronted. Three brash villains invaded, and only later would I learn they were ages fifteen and seventeen. The first crawled through the kitchen window, while the others awaited to prey from the shadows.

Our four children were aged two to six. What soon befell me spared them, or else this story would be unbearable, not writable from this young mother. Being home alone had never bothered me, even though our flanking neighborhood, away from the traffic on the backside, seemed at times a bit shady. Perhaps naïve, I had never feared for our safety.

On the second night of my husband's absence, the opening of the back door awoke me. I immediately confronted three hooded men with covered faces. They demanded money, but I had none in the house. The previous week, I had paid some bills too early, jeopardizing our account balances, which had prompted me to gather every last coin for an emergency deposit. The episode took its most sordid turn when they realized my husband was gone. Robbery transitioned to one hour of violation.

After agreeing not to bother our sleeping children, two of them searched the house. Meanwhile, the third invader, the largest and eldest, took me to another part of the house and forced me to remove my clothes, then to perform sexual acts on him. When the other two returned, they joined the first, raping me numerous times in a few different rooms. All the while, the threat rang out that any word, then or later, and they'd kill our children—returning if needed.

Our bodies produce adrenaline during such crises. It fuels our survival mode—and any evidence contrary is hard for me to reconcile with those several hours. No thoughts of fighting back or running away, or any actions that would increase the chance that these men would harm my babies. I had to stay. To endure. To gratify greed. To experience their reprobate absence of remorse. To tolerate cowardice of the highest order. To stare sin face-on (or at the least what was visible above their hiked up hoodies). I became determined. "Whatever it takes, whatever it costs, whatever the sacrifice to leave us alone."

I prayed aloud that Jesus would watch over our children; that he would keep them asleep in the midst of encroaching hands of evil. At one point,

I could see into our master bedroom where our four-year-old daughter had been sleeping with me earlier. God kept her eyes closed, her sleep peaceful, as one of the intruders rummaged dresser drawers right next to her—with the lights on. My prayers would continue until they finally left. Prayers not just for my kids, but also for these guys. That they would somehow find Jesus through this experience. That they would stop. That I would have wisdom to respond appropriately.

Their deviousness surfaced anew. As they gathered all our electronics, they forced me to bathe. Two even took our van for an outing, delivered their booty, and then returned it to join the intrusion anew. When they were finally satisfied, they ordered me to shut the door behind them, with their final words being "have a blessed night." The rest of the night passed slowly, an extended stupor, with no way to contact anyone. To go to neighbors meant leaving our kids alone. Perhaps there was no right decision, and those hours prolonged what appeared at times to be an out-of-body experience.

As morning finally broke, rays of hope illuminated my heart and home. I made the kids' breakfast and got them dressed, and then we went to find my husband. Before leaving, I told them about being robbed, that some bad people needed money so they took our things, and that we had to go tell Daddy. They were so resilient. Upon calling Simon out of class, the kids greeted him with, "We were robbed!" Miraculously, I had already arranged play dates for all of them for first thing that morning.

As their childlike stories unfolded, Simon started connecting the dots— that I had interacted with the intruders. We stepped away from the kids, and I directed him to ask questions to which I could answer yes or no. After only a few inquiries, every husband's deep fear shone on his face. Then he did the only thing I needed him to do; he held me. And for the first time since the ordeal began, I allowed myself to cry. I knew that I was safe.

He called the police immediately and met them at our house. The next few days unfolded with beauty, even amidst the taxing police interviews.

I felt the world had my back. The media had carried considerable details nationwide, which in some ways removed that decision from me. Our neighbors knew. Our friends knew. It seemed the whole world knew.

The body of Christ poured out love and prayers, and I know God heard those prayers. Friends housed us as needed. Our parents came to help with the kids. Within the first day, someone offered to pay for temporary housing while we looked for a new place to live. A friend bought our current home, so we didn't have to worry about selling it—or being in it.

Two days after the incident, we were staying with friends out in the country in a home perfectly secluded to provide the respite we needed. One of my best friends called and asked if she, her husband, and their boys could come see us. She wanted to hug me, and he had something he needed to tell us. Simon's parents watched all the kids by the pool as the couple took us aside. The husband looked at us and plainly stated, "I received a call today and there is an anonymous donor that wants to buy you a house. Any house you want."

Simon simply turned, walked a few steps away, and his body began to tremble with sobs. How could we cry tears of such great pain and immense gratitude only forty-eight hours apart? We were in a state of great ambivalence. (Wherever the donor is, we hope they realize that they have been the hands and feet of Christ that helped make a hurting family whole again.)

We were at our worst, and yet could feel the greatest joy through God's outpouring of love through believers. Physical possessions are not heavenly treasures, but God knows we need them. I have no doubt that at times he uses them to bless and help restore us. Over the months that followed, I was overwhelmed and humbled with the continued financial gifts, as well as the words of encouragement and prayers.

My husband had the wits about him to help detectives immediately track our laptop, and just in time—before it was electronically disengaged. More than a month after the break-in, the intruders were all arrested, with fingerprints and DNA matches confirming identities. Heartbreakingly, they were arrested while at their high school. The legal process is far from over, but my hope is that my testimony helps prevent these men from repeating their actions. And our journey will help others when they confront the worst of man's fallen nature.

How does God fit into such a story? I can only surmise that if God can allow something this bad to happen and then bring so much good out of it, I have full hope that my life is OK in his hands. That whatever else he allows me to go through, he'll be there in the midst of it and will work it out for his glory. I sometimes wrestle with. "But God was supposed to be my protector!" But another question could be, "Why was I allowed to live when many Christians are dying cruel deaths?" There are unlimited questions, but most are not for my story. And that's key; we all have journeys and each is important.

I've resigned to the reality that I'll not know until heaven the degree to which God was watching over us that night. Did he keep the children asleep. Was Simon's rare absence actually what spared his life? Perhaps if I had fought back I would have been maimed. The "what ifs" can drive someone crazy if allowed the space.

People voiced visceral reactions, such as, "That is my worst fear; I would never survive." Or "My life would be over!" The challenge is not to allow another's sin to create fear in your heart. I am *alive* in Christ. The same God who got us through this is the same God who is with you in your life's story.

GRACE FOR US ALL

CHERIE (ROLOSON) HORST

Editor's Note: One lesson becomes evident in the story below: just because you've endured a hard situation, or a stretch of them, doesn't mean you've navigated your quota for this life. I can imagine Cherie and her husband, Steve, pausing many times and asking God, "Why us?" Or, "Is this fair after what we've already been through?" Life isn't one of scoreboards, and certainly not of quotas.

For many years I served in upper administration at the college where Steve is a professor, and a good one at that. However, he seemed to have a tough time wrapping up his dissertation. The months became years, and years nearly a decade. He's brilliant, industrious, and an extremely positive person steeped in magnetic humility. It wasn't until reading this story that I began to connect the dots and to applaud all the more that he's now Dr. Horst with a book coming soon with ACU Press.

In his providence, does God hone our personal characteristics and strengths through trials that will one day help others, especially our children? It seems to have worked out well that two young girls were adopted by a couple with the capacity to understand them and love them. While Cherie finds God's continuing grace in a baby named Grace, I see God's grace also in a mother named Cherie and a remarkably consistent husband named Dr. Steve Horst.

▼ ▼ ▼

When I was twenty, the world looked a lot different than it does to me now at sixty. My life took quite a different path than I had imagined from the dreamy slopes of youth. From that perch, I could see myself marrying a Christian, probably a pastor's son, as I was pastor's daughter. I assumed we would have a few children of our own and then maybe adopt a few needy kids. We would then have a wonderful life of family and ministry. I envisioned a life like Jo's in Louisa May Alcott's *Little Men*.

Not that my childhood had been exemplary. Though an only child until age eleven when my parents adopted an infant, my life was far from the nuclear family espoused on *Focus on the Family*. We moved nine times in my twelve years of public school, our "homes" scattered across five different states. My mother's bipolar illness complicated our tenuous stability. I don't think many would fault me for my deep desire for a neat and tidy family life, though I feared becoming a parent if there was any chance of becoming a mercurial mother like mine.

I did marry a pastor's son, and he's a wonderful husband, but the dream ended there.

After reassurance from several doctors that I was not bipolar, I pursued the idea of having children. When I did not get pregnant by age thirty, fertility specialists at Loyola University Hospital diagnosed me with advanced endometriosis. Childbearing would be difficult if not impossible, but I set my face like a flint, determined to complete the long battery of special tests and undergo the prescribed remedial surgeries. "Lord, how long?" we cried.

After years of futile efforts, we explored adoption. But here we found ourselves in another complex, confusing maze. Expect a three-year wait, we were told. And the cost? Nearly double our annual income. Then I struggled with a hesitancy provoked from my childhood. My adopted younger sister's likes, dislikes, tastes, and even biorhythms always seemed out of sync with our immediate family. My husband and I weren't ready to "sign on" for infant adoption. Yet, having been married nearly twelve years, we knew our hope for a child was diminishing monthly.

But then friends suggested another option: adopting a foster child. They had done so and we'd thought we'd consider this—eventually, after gaining experience with our own children. But now we began thinking alternatively that perhaps God wanted us to try our hand at foster parenting first. We appreciated the benefits of a "trial" period; if a child didn't work out, she could be assigned to a different home. Aware of the risks and rewards, we began foster parenting classes and the home study in early 1990. A new chapter of our family life began when Bess arrived at our house for a half-day visit.

Bess had been in the system for a while. Though her mother had been mentally compromised since birth, Bess was bright, articulate, and in need of care. She had thrived in her first foster home before going to live with her father. When that didn't work out, her former foster family was not available. Would we be interested?

Bess very much reminded me of my little sister—the sister I felt I had "abandoned" to attend college. I hadn't been able to save my sister from an unstable home, but I could "save" this beautiful child, Bess.

What a joyful time of life it was for me. After getting much-needed glasses, Bess responded quickly by reading books. And she could pick up songs by ear, playing our old piano. But I knew the loneliness of being an only child. Bess needed a companion. We wanted a fuller house so we welcomed four-year-old Sandy into our home in 1991.

Sandy and Bess were almost complete opposites. While Bess was confident, exuberant, outspoken, and daring, Sandy was quiet, withdrawn, secretive, and angry. She claimed she "didn't need another mother"—me—because her own mother loved her and needed her. Of course she didn't understand the complications of her original home, including a loving, but needy, mother who had been mentally disabled in a childhood car accident. Bess, two years older, was great with Sandy and took her under her wing. "You call them Mom and Dad," she told Sandy. "I'll show you what to do."

After Sandy had been with us more than three years, we received a surprising phone call from the social worker. She had picked Sandy up from school and was taking her for a psychological evaluation. This was a lot like the day she'd been removed from her biological mother: no notice, simply picked up and taken away to our home. We'd hardly realized what trauma she'd been through. Now we wondered if Sandy was being removed from our home. Had our plans to move become an issue?

As we prayed for a smooth adoption of Sandy, we also prayed for it be expeditious, as we had been appointed by The Wesleyan Church as missionaries to Russia. With the psychologist's recommendation for a speedy adoption, the judge made a ruling and declared Sandra Marie legally our daughter on May 9, 1995. We soon left for Russia on schedule with all passports and visas in hand. At last, our family was settled: a three-year appointment halfway around the world. Or so we thought.

Within the year, I suddenly lost sight in my right eye, forcing us to move back to Indianapolis (to The Wesleyan Church Headquarters). Medical tests quickly resulted in a shocking diagnosis: multiple sclerosis (MS). Reality set in: we couldn't return to a difficult mission field. If you've been forced to make an about-face with a major life goal, you know how difficult such a transition can be. We put one foot in front of the other. For Bess, we brought one bit of Russia into our Indiana sphere. Our time in Russia had enhanced her piano skills. Upon our return, we continued with Russian piano teachers, one of them a concert pianist. She said Bess was capable of going to Julliard if she chose.

We were excited that Indiana Wesleyan University hired Steve, though Sandy, now age fourteen, wasn't happy with the move to the small-town of Marion. She'd been in the Indianapolis Children's Choir and loved our church. She'd asked to be baptized. The move was a culture shock; she found "tractor day" an odd school tradition, when seniors arrived on their family tractors. And was she really the only one in her social studies class who didn't know of a family member involved with the KKK? Eventually and fortunately, she found a place in drama and won the role of Liesel in the production of *The Sound of Music*. She loved it! But our home was anything but tranquil.

Just as Sandy seemed to find herself, Bess was losing ground, eventually diagnosed with a bipolar disorder. The very disease I had feared inheriting from my own mother was now creating havoc in our home, afflicting our dear Bess. She did well when she took her meds, and soon enough she enrolled as a freshman at St. Mary of the Woods Catholic University, entering their music theory program.

Sandy's senior year seemed to be going well; she was acting in several school plays, competing with the speech team, and maintaining good grades. She was taking college credits "in escrow" while working at McDonald's. She'd been accepted at Huntington University in their drama program.

And then, in March, Sandy became nauseous for two days. When we came home from a Bible study and she was still vomiting profusely, I took her to the ER. After giving her an IV, taking blood samples and X-rays, poking and prodding extensively, a doctor asked me to step out of the room for a minute. Standing in the hall, I had second thoughts. "She's still a minor; I should be with her!" As I walked back into the room, the doctor said, "Oh, good. You're here. I've just informed Sandy that she's pregnant." The doctor then turned and left me standing there, dumbfounded.

Sandy wasn't dating, though I knew she'd been casually interested in several young men. For the past two days, I'd repeatedly asked if there was any way she could be pregnant. No, she said. Even before the X-ray had been taken, when being advised of the possible danger to a fetus, she denied any possibility. But the doctor said otherwise.

How was this possible? She was our star child, a "good Christian," active in youth group. We were so excited about the new world that was about to open up for her when she went to college. At first, I spoke out of anger and frustration: "You've really messed up your life. How could you have been so foolish?" I may have used stronger words. Then I said, "I'd better go, before I say more," and walked out.

Waiting for the elevator, looking down at my wrist, I saw my WWJD bracelet. "OK, Jesus, what would you do if this happened to you?" I said, almost defiantly. Then in a gentle voice, I heard him say, "I'd tell her I love her." As the elevator door opened, I turned around and went back to Sandy's room. I held out my arms to her and said, "I love you." She fell into my arms sobbing, and I held fast to her.

Of course that great bonding moment was not the end of the story. We had to make decisions. Sandy called the father and told him the news. They talked of marriage, but we reminded her that she was not yet eighteen, and we were in no hurry for her to make a second mistake. When she was of age in a few months, she could evaluate what she wanted to do. She told us that in those few brief moments at the hospital, the doctor had mentioned abortion. She had emphatically said no. Hearing this news, I sensed her bravery and told her I was proud of her.

In the months that followed, Sandy was reunited with her birth mother. For the first time, Sandy saw the extent of her mother's cognitive disabilities. Now she understood my explanation given since childhood. "Your mother loves you very much, but she just could not adequately take care of you."

As the pregnancy progressed, Sandy gained clarity and chose not to get married. The father signed off on his rights, giving Sandy full responsibility and also the freedom to choose how best to handle the situation, including adoption. Feeling the gravity of looming parenthood at seventeen, she asked me, "How am I going to do this?"

And I said, "Grace! God's grace will get us through." And so that became the baby's name: Grace, for all of God's provisions, and Marie as a middle name, as that was Sandy's middle name.

Sandy continued with her plans to attend Huntington University in the fall. She lived at home with us and commuted daily, while also attending birthing classes. Sandy asked me to be her birthing coach, and each night we sang "Amazing Grace" to little Grace Marie.

At 5:30 one morning, Sandy's water broke. We immediately headed off to the hospital, expecting a long day. But after just two pushes, Grace Marie was born. "There she is," I exclaimed, and she turned her head toward me as if she recognized my voice from all those evenings of talking and singing to her.

After Gracie was born, Sandy asked if Steve and I would legally adopt Gracie as our third child. Sandy transferred to Indiana Wesleyan University that year and graduated in 2009. She continued to live at home until she married in 2010. Now we share Gracie with Sandy. It's complicated and sometimes messy. But we continue to seek God's guidance for loving these three girls as Jesus would. And we are indeed proud parents.

Sometimes we get it right, and sometimes we don't. But there is grace for all of us.

HOPE BRINGS HEALING

MARILYN SIMONS

Editor's Note: One of the favorite gathering spots for large groups from our church has been Marilyn's majestic house—with its yard and woods, alongside a creek, even a gorgeous pool that seems to blend in with the natural surroundings. The tree swing and bonfire areas were always favorites. And at summer evening gatherings, Marilyn's laugh echoed across the lawns. Somehow trips to Marilyn's helped people set aside their troubles and find retreat. That's still true, though the landscape has changed a bit. The great swing and bonfire areas are now owned by another—her former husband, who received half the property during their divorce and is building his home there. The parties aren't as frequent, as kids are adults now and many live elsewhere. But through all of this, Marilyn still can smile wide and laugh deeply. Perhaps because what she shares below is of a sensitive matter that often is shared only between women, or perhaps because I just wasn't as attentive to the needs of a good friend . . . I wasn't aware of the underlying issue in her life—childhood sexual abuse—until I helped her edit a grant proposal for a project to educate the wider community. I'm glad she's in a good place and can laugh loud, and that she's a testimony that no matter how abused or oppressed, we can find joy in the morning.

▼ ▼ ▼

This is my story. It's not pretty, but it is headed toward a happy ending. I'll skip a lot of the details and trust the candor helps.

When I was six years old, a close relative sexually abused me. This event alone shook my life to the core. In addition, my family had few boundaries, compounding my situation. Most parents are not prepared to deal with such harsh violations. I suppose mine managed the best they could, but in the end they did not attend to my needs.

In some ways, the abuse seemed inevitable—though it never is, and we should work to combat it. My father was physically abused as a child and my mother sexually abused as well. The harshest irony is that the one person who actually seemed to care for me, eventually sexually abused me. Though the abuse was short-lived, the effects were not, and the scars stretch to the present.

I've also learned that some hardships result from sin and others from being human. Just when I finally met the man I would marry, I had to deal with a hysterectomy, though I was only thirty-five years old. The romance seemed like a fairy tale when, three years later, I walked the aisle at a beautiful wedding.

I'm thankful for those early years of our marriage, but about ten years later I dejectedly walked down the courthouse hallway, divorced. The previous five years had been riddled with the physical trauma of biopsies and multiple medical procedures, then the official diagnosis of breast cancer.

It's a bit dizzying to think back to those painful years. My second major surgery (completing a double mastectomy) occurred between my husband's filing for divorce and its completion. Just a few months later, my mom died. My father followed just two years after that. The next year, the widow of my brother died. Within the same week, in the same church, we had funerals for twin relatives, just infants.

During this onslaught of crises, I tried to anticipate joy: some of my favorite relatives were going to move in with me. The downside included the construction logistics of building a high-end, separate living space on the bottom level of my home—complete with a view of the woods and the bluff over the creek.

The next few years were filled with new life around my house and such joy. With no kids of my own, I had an abundance of love to pour into the lives of my relatives, especially the children. But sometimes familiarity breeds contempt, and we parted ways, relationships broken that still break my heart.

Other family failures added worry. However—and this is where my own abuse comes full circle—my ongoing concern was for younger relatives who needed assistance. As a healthcare professional with an advanced degree, and with considerable experience in helping others with crises, I've been strategically placed to try to make sure that the next generation is carefully monitored while in the care of my abuser. My hope and prayer is that the cycle of abuse is broken.

Family dynamics are constant reminders that my life's primary defining issue was and will continue to be sexual abuse. The next defining issues, not that I can really think of these being separated were being barren and divorced.

You've read quite a sad journey, but there is hope. In the late 1990s, my personal life was falling apart. I struggled with self-loathing. I was clinically depressed and could hardly get off of the couch. With the help of some friends relentlessly involved, I found a counselor who was the right fit for me. I had been to counselors before. This time it was different. Not to make light of it, but it's sort of like the first visit between Bob Wiley (Bill Murray) and Dr. Leo Marvin in Touchstone Picture's *What about Bob?* That is, for Bob, the lights went on; after years of sessions with other doctors, he finally found help. In my case, after the first visit with the new person, I realized I had been sexually abused. Before that time, everyone told me that what happened to me was normal. Unlike with Bob, there was nothing funny. Though my personality and relationship with friends would help me laugh and have fun at times, the lingering child-hood trauma always overshadowed me. But finally, I was seeing it for what it was.

Sexual abuse is not normal!

At first the healing from sexual abuse was a full-time and very painful journey. I regularly went to the personal counselor and group counseling. I feverishly wrote in my journal. I read every self-help book I thought would make a difference for me. My medicines for depression were changed and increased. I prayed more than ever before and felt God's presence more acutely than at any other time in my life.

The insights of books served as a lifeline, especially *On the Threshold of Hope* by Diane Langberg, which I read cover to cover about ten times in two days. I stayed home from work so I could continue reading. Finally, I had resources to explain my feelings and behavior. I was not an awful person; I was a person reacting to childhood sexual abuse.

This is my song.

I am on the other side of sexual abuse and the other defining moments in my life. I am still in the healing process, and perhaps this season will be long. God is alive and active in my life. The wound of not being able to have my own children has healed as I experienced a personal rebirth. I am learning that being reborn in Christ is the best—even better than having children of my own.

God is wonderful and I sing his praises. With God's help, I can now help others who have been sexually abused. I have traveled to three coun-tries to share about my experience and how God has healed me. God then helps others to heal. Regardless of any legal steps we need to help people in dealing with their abuse, there will also always be the need for healing.

While others are better positioned to educate on the former, and it's an important part of the journey to recovery, God has positioned me to help with the latter.

There is no greater song than surviving a seemingly impossible defining moment and having God heal the wounds, and then being able to help others.

Now I can praise my Jesus "all the day long."

THE FLIPSIDE OF DESPAIR

JACK ROBINSON

Editor's Note: *Christians often talk about the old life before Christ and the new one, with him. One of our most enduring hymns is "Amazing Grace."[1] It has memorialized the flipside of being lost with that singular phrase "but now am found." We all sing in unison about being "a wretch," and we can do so because God's grace has enveloped us. It has helped us to find joy, purpose, hope, and a host of other positive aspects of being alive. Jack Robinson knows this reality well and has been rather transparent in reflecting on the transition from his old to new self. In this book, we feature a few people who have dealt with this sense of feeling utterly lost, a sense of hopelessness that prompts them to want to escape some emotional abyss. But we also realize that we'd likely not even know these people had they not held on to life and reached for a new dawn. And we'd certainly not be able to value their stories of hope and meaning.*

▼   ▼   ▼

The darkness of my despair eclipsed any glimmer of hope. Light simply didn't seem to pierce my world until one fateful day when I attempted to end it all. Thank God, I lived. I lived and immediately thanked God. Have you ever been in such a depressive state? If so, perhaps this will be a helpful reflection. If not—and I'm glad if you're in this camp—I hope that my story helps you understand people bowed down by such challenges.

The day of my attempted suicide will remain a defining moment until I reach heaven.

While driving on a Sunday afternoon, I aligned my Jeep directly in the path of an oncoming semitrailer. After unbuckling my seatbelt, I accelerated. Seeing my approach, the semi driver hurled his rig into a ditch, as I drove on by, escaping lethal impact. I was numb. After reaching an abandoned house trailer, I cried out, "God, why is this happening to me?"

What happened next may be even more difficult to believe. I felt someone tap my shoulder and say, "You're at a crossroads in your life. Choose right now what you're going to do." Simultaneously, I saw a vision of a person's right hand with a picture of my father in it. God was saying, "This isn't really a picture of your father, but of you, if you continue living the way you are." I also saw a left hand with no promises other than that I would not become like my father—a drunk. This was my choice.

My personal road to that bout with the semi was bumpy, to say the least. I grew up in a rather dysfunctional family with five siblings, an alcoholic father, and a bread-winning mother who required us to go to church so she could have some respite. But those Sabbaths led not to worship, but to disenchantment with Christianity. The legalistic hellfire and brimstone preaching was a one-sided rant on joy. God's grace and mercy weren't anywhere in the preacher's sermonic mix, and I suppose it is little wonder that I constantly struggled to live by the rules.

Lack of self-esteem didn't help, a result of parents who said I would never amount to anything. If my parents didn't love me, how could God? After graduating from high school, I left my parents' house. It was an effort to escape the guilt of falling short of everybody's rules.

I joined people like me trying to fill their lives with fake substitutes for God, particularly alcohol and drugs. The tentacles of these alluring addictions followed me to the military. Perhaps the one sane exuberant release from the daily dose was bicycle road racing with friends.

As I somehow took on more duties as an Air Force specialist with top-secret security clearance working on nuclear bombs, I *had* to keep my drinking under control. In 1983, after completing military service and working a variety of jobs, I married a young woman with two children.

But the addictions again captivated me, jeopardizing my work and my marriage. In 1989 my wife divorced me, and I floundered. Losing all self-confidence, I allowed the addictions to gain ground. With no place to call home, sleeping at friends' houses or in my Jeep, I saw suicide as my way out, to erase and relieve the pain.

Before that semi driver thwarted my suicide attempt, I had visited my mother and stepfather, looking for some small measure of hope and comfort. But what I found wasn't enough. Guilt and despair were suffocating me.

After that moment, I began the long road to full recovery. The following Thursday, I entered treatment, followed by years with Alcoholics Anonymous (AA). From learning many Scriptures, and with the constant support of Christian men at AA, I came to believe in the full, eternal power of Christ and have remained sober ever since.

It's perhaps illogical how we develop and break habits and addictions. Even though God miraculously delivered me from alcoholism, I avoided church for some time. I didn't want to be seen as a hypocrite, unable to keep all the rules. It took another thirteen years before I regularly attended church again, after marrying Gail in 1999.

Gail's coworker invited us to her church. I knew immediately that God was calling me back to himself. I couldn't wait for the altar call the following week. And at that altar, God's amazing transformation in my life began.

I've come to understand my worth and value before God, who became very real to me. One day, while remodeling a bathroom, I felt God hug me, just as a father would his son. God put my life on a new trajectory. I pray and read the Bible daily. Even my personal finances have turned around. The practice of tithing seemed simultaneous with stability. We've never been hungry or late on bills. It's hard to capture how great life is, even with tough times that we all face.

Today I work as a maintenance electrician in a wire mill. My daily hope is to try to let the life-transforming work of Jesus Christ quietly flow from my life. Our daughter and son-in-law are missionaries in Uganda. I hope our four dearly loved grandchildren, who call me Poppi, will remember me as a man of God who became everything God created me to be. I hope to be remembered as a man who, as bad as things were earlier in life, found God and was found by God, and never refused to give up. My life is testimony that God doesn't give up on us.

NOTE

1. John Newton, "Amazing Grace," 1779, public domain.

STRANGER AT MY DOOR

TINA GOODPASTER

Editor's Note: Life can sure throw us curves. Some people manage to hit home runs during these times and others struggle. Unfortunately, too many either strike out or feel helplessly exposed. Whatever the outcome, these times of crisis help define us. More important, they help us learn about God and his promises. While he offers hope, sometimes in overtly miraculous ways, as in the story below, we can fail to recognize it or choose to ignore positive possibilities. For some, the question becomes not how to survive but whether surviving is worth the cost. Much heroic literature captures someone's passionate quest to survive or someone's willingness to risk living to keep another from dying. The writers of these classics capture part of what is quintessentially human, the will to live. Against this backdrop, it's tough to comprehend the depth of despair that drives one to suicide. Sometimes it's a chemical imbalance or destructive chemical poisoning. But sometimes it's tied to those curves that seem to leave us exposed at home plate. The list of possibilities is long. Exhausted from striking out. Drained from the prolonged battle. Embarrassed. Ashamed. Out of resources for help to overcome. The following story affords a glimpse of this struggle. Tina's transparency reveals both the pressures that bring about faulty but felt logic, and also God's provisions even in their midst. We find her thankful for a God who draws close to the brokenhearted.

▼ ▼ ▼

While my two young children were at their dad's for the weekend, I was home contemplating the benefits of ending my life. Divorced for several years, I felt I was at the end of my rope as a single mother. Being a Christian didn't seem to help, nor did attending church. My family lived in another state, and I felt painfully alone on Sundays as I left the sanctuary.

Dating was a dead end as well. I had gone through a series of toxic relationships in desperate attempts to mend my heart and household. Each relationship's termination left me simultaneously emptier and carrying even more shame.

Late one afternoon, while sitting in my kitchen, I surmised that, by ending my life, my young children would be able to live with their father and bond with their stepmother. Eventually their memories of me would be faint at best. Yes, a clean break for them at an early age might be best. I reached for but could not grasp a positive thought, since I was obviously not equipped to be a parent. Or so I reasoned. They didn't need to grow up broken because I had failed. This was twisted logic at best, but it made perfect sense to me that day. I began to consider suicidal options—not *if* but *how*.

These thoughts captivated me and in a dizzying stupor I picked up my dishes, intending to wash them. I had designed my kitchen to feature a window above the sink where I could look out over a field across the street. Here I did my best thinking. Standing there at the sink, I noticed a car drive by slowly, through my field of vision. The male driver and I made eye contact. Thinking it odd but not giving it much attention, I returned to my macabre contemplation. A couple of minutes later, a car pulled into the driveway and a man knocked on my door.

Of course I was suspicious and annoyed. "What does he want? Why now, when I'm working through 'plans'?" But I reluctantly answered the door, intending to dismiss him quickly.

He introduced himself as a pastor from a church in another county. I immediately recognized him as the guest preacher at a campground we visited. "Do you know Jesus?" he asked. Having been raised in church, I knew what he wanted to hear and what would make him go away. Only he didn't go away. This campground preacher was relentless. He continued to stand on my porch lobbing a wave of questions about my relationship with God, prompting me to continue returning more "right answers." As dusk approached and the wind turned chilly, Preacher-man showed no intent of leaving, so I reluctantly invited him in.

The rest of the story is blurry but remains an important reflection. Sitting at the table where minutes earlier I had been pondering ways to end my life, I blurted out my life story to a stranger. I cried as I mentioned my current, damaging relationship with a man, which I felt powerless to end. The preacher didn't reply with any particularly profound theology; rather, he described the type of life he wished for me if I were his daughter. Suddenly I recognized God's voice through this pastor. God, through him, spoke to me as his daughter and revealed his heart and plans for me and my children's hopeful future. God's love broke through my despair.

After we prayed and he began to leave, I couldn't help but ask how he discovered my address. The campground didn't track drive-in guests, and many were from out of town. I had not introduced myself, so he could not have looked me up in the phone book, even if God had prompted him. I was genuinely perplexed.

His answer would become an eternal memorial of God's faithfulness. He had driven to my city (Marion, Indiana) to visit a family that had attended his church and requested a visit. Although he had confirmed plans to visit before making the drive, no one was home. After waiting for some time, he decided to leave and head back to his place.

He was feeling quite frustrated with the wasted trip, but, just as he came upon our street, he felt impressed to "turn here." Not knowing our town or where our street led, he trusted God and came down our street, praying, "Lord, you need to show me exactly where I need to go." His first stop was at the address next door to me, a one-story apartment complex. When every door he knocked on was not answered or closed in his face, he returned to his car and drove farther. That's when he looked over and saw me at my kitchen window. After stopping at my neighbor's on the other side with no success, he came back and pulled into my driveway.

The moment I opened the door, God confirmed in his spirit: "This is it." When I lobbed all the "right answers" at him, God did not release him to leave, so he kept talking, even when the sun started to set and the wind turned cold. He had made plans that day, but God had directed his steps to my door and he stayed.

That day, despair was forever transformed to hope. My family began learning to see, hear, and trust God's love. Today, over fifteen years later, I am married to a loving man, and my children are grown. God performed a miracle through this man's obedience that saved my life and preserved my family. Although I still encounter doubt, my journey of learning to see, hear, and trust God's love continues! Our family is still on that road that the pastor said he would wish for his own daughter.

Perhaps the risk of being transparent here is countered by the likelihood that someone reading this might be sinking into despair, staring at beauty outside the window but seeing no possible route to its enjoyment, seeing only a bleak future. Although God may not send a preacher to knock at your door, I know that he will be there. In some form, he is always there. Always. Perhaps this very story is that needed interruption.

"For he has rescued us from the dominion of darkness and brought us into the kingdom of the Son he loves" (Col. 1:13).

LOSING TO GAIN MYSELF

KIM MILLER

Editor's note: From The Biggest Loser *to diet books, we're reminded often of a struggle many of us go through at some point. When at the beach, our four boys looked at me in a wet shirt and said I looked like a shrink-wrapped pear. That was twenty years ago and I'm afraid I still battle with this issue. At least I'm now counting steps daily, though, despite my efforts, I struggle to meet the minimum ten thousand. Kim Miller's story reminds me of the depths of this struggle, not just for herself, but also for millions of others. Even Rick Warren has raised awareness with his book,* The Daniel Plan: 40 Days to a Healthier Life *and ancillary diet books. Many readers find it hard to separate dietary benefits from spiritual gains. Kim writes with a transparency that at first might feel uncomfortable, what our boys refer to as TMI or "too much information." But within a few paragraphs it becomes clear that she includes this nearly unbelievable list of ailments as a way to accent her amazing recovery.*

▼   ▼   ▼

It almost sounds cliché, but as a middle-aged professional I found a complete transformation through weight loss. And complete is just that:

from the physical, to the emotional, and even the spiritual. During my journey to a healthy self, Romans 8:25 took on special meaning: "If we hope for what we do not see, with perseverance we wait eagerly for it" (NASB). I suppose you might say I was hoping not to see what was always there in every mirror, in storefront windows as I walked by, and every morning when I dressed for the day.

In the fall of 2011, I wasn't feeling eager about anything. Life had hit hard in recent years. I had lost my dad after his prolonged battle with leukemia. My father-in-law was gravely ill. My husband and I had uprooted from our home of twenty years for a seemingly wonderful job opportunity for me—teaching accounting—that turned out to be unexpectedly demanding. My life no longer felt familiar, and I wasn't sure we had made the right decision in leaving a supportive community. My faith, normally solid, wavered.

As my stress increased, so did the number on the scales. After long struggles to manage my weight, I reached a point where I just stopped trying. More than ever, I turned to food for emotional support. I found myself physically ill, extremely fatigued, deeply depressed, and morbidly obese. It was a challenge to drag myself to work each morning. I constantly felt sick and in pain. It was all I could do to make it through the day and come home to collapse on the couch, where I spent most evenings. I was not who I wanted to be, but I didn't know what to do about it. I didn't even know how to pray. I just cried out to God for help.

Leading up to that point, I was undergoing treatment for a number of issues: hypothyroidism, irritable bowel syndrome (IBS), adrenal fatigue, gastroesophageal reflux disease (GERD), and uterine fibroids. I realize that even listing these paints an uninviting picture of myself. Suffice it to say, I wasn't well. With the help of a number of medications, however, I thought it was manageable.

In October 2011, my doctor strongly urged me to take an immediate leave of absence from work so that my ailments could be better addressed.

Ever self-sufficient and strongly stubborn, I wouldn't even consider it. I was right in the middle of a semester. I couldn't do that to my students or my department. Besides, it wasn't *that* bad. I think I looked at self-care as a sort of self-indulgence so I soldiered on.

But when my father-in-law passed away in January 2012, I reached the end of myself. I knew I did not have the strength to face another semester and I needed to heed the doctor's advice. I took a leave of absence and underwent a barrage of tests that detected an intestinal parasite, leaky gut, food sensitivities, an inability to metabolize certain vitamins, hormonal imbalances, and prediabetes.

Change is hard and old habits don't die easily. Each day was a battle. Having first addressed the parasite issue, the next step was eliminating certain foods from my diet. For about three weeks, I experienced sugar withdrawal symptoms that made me feel even worse. Temptation taunted me. I fought, cried, resisted, and rebelled. Many days I wanted to give up. Food had become my comfort, and, quite frankly, I enjoyed it.

In those trying times, something beautiful developed. I learned to rely on others and accept help. God taught me about community. He placed precious people in my path, just when I needed them. First and foremost, there was my family—strongly supportive and always believing in me. Then there was my patient medical team—my tenacious doctor, counselor, and nutritionist. My doctor also referred me to specialists, as needed. In addition, I was privileged to work with five extraordinary students at Taylor University, who were my personal trainers over the next few years. Last, I was buoyed by an accountability group—friends who met once a week to encourage each other to live healthfully.

Incremental physical transformation took place: pound by pound, inch by inch. I celebrated every tiny victory. Within a year, I had lost fifty pounds. Other measures also improved—cholesterol, blood pressure, and glucose levels. More important, I was being healed emotionally and spiritually.

Hope budded and I started to feel like myself again. I know in my heart that my struggle with weight was a spiritual battle as much as it was physical. Satan did not want me to be well. He wanted me to continue to be a slave to food—to be despondent, despairing, and hopeless. In that condition, I was unable to give God my best. In that condition, I had no energy, no optimism, and no self-confidence. I knew only shame and self-doubt. That was not the life that God wanted for me. So God gave me the courage and the power to fight my way out of it.

Transformation is liberating. It is going from not being able to run even a quarter of a mile, to running in races—five 5-Ks, a 10-K, a 15-K, a 3-mile, a 6-mile, and a 10-mile, to date. And guess what's coming soon? Yep, a half marathon! Transformation means a whole new wardrobe. It means being able to have dance parties with my granddaughters, being full of energy, and able to pass up a chocolate brownie and not crave it even a little bit. It even means having a whole new outlook on life and being overwhelmed with gratitude.

In two and a half years, I lost 120 pounds.

When I look at my before and after pictures, I marvel at the difference. I am astonished and amazed, because I know that the change is so much more than just physical. A key biblical promise stayed with me: "A bruised reed he will not break, and a smoldering wick he will not snuff out" (Isa. 42:3). I was a bruised reed that God protected and held tenderly. I was the smoldering wick that God would not allow to be extinguished. I know with absolute assurance that God rescued me. My heart overflows with joy as I think about all that he has done for me.

My journal is replete with reflections on God's promises, such as Leviticus 26:13: "I am the LORD your God, who brought you out of Egypt so that you would no longer be slaves to the Egyptians; I broke the bars of your yoke and enabled you to walk with heads held high." My recorded thoughts on this passage include the following:

"This passage speaks to me about my latest journey—my journey to health. I was a slave to food and unhealthy eating habits. God released me—he broke the bars of that heavy yoke so that I can walk free, 'head held high.' I love that imagery! *Praise you, Father! You rescued me. You showed me a better way. You were tender and patient with me. You told me how precious I am to you and how much you value and love me. You have truly given me new life.*"

Not only has God given me new life; he has given me a new calling. I feel so liberated by my experience that I now have a burning passion to help others in similar situations. I am currently training to become a Certified Health and Wellness Coach. It's a drastic change from Certified Public Accountant, but I know that God is a God of transformations, and I am very excited for the opportunity that he has placed before me.

I have made Romans 8:25 my theme verse for this year. Filled with hope, I wait eagerly to see what God will do next in my life! And now my focus isn't so much on me or what one sees or doesn't see, but about others and what God will allow me to see in them, and how I might be used to help.

PART 4

THE TRUTH OF GOD'S PRESENCE

THE NIGHT JANITOR

DAVID DRURY

Editor's Note: Malcolm Gladwell's ten-thousand-hour thesis comes to mind with the story below. In his bestselling book Outliers, *he presents a convincing notion that the elite athletes, musicians, and other professionals have logged at least ten thousand hours on tasks related to their careers. This includes people like Bill Gates and the hours spent on computer programming early in his career. In his story, below, David Drury gives a glimpse of why he surfaced at a young age as a leader in local churches and on the national stage. And why he began assisting some outstanding thinkers, such as Max Lucado and Steve DeNeff, with their books. Oh, he didn't intend this story for this purpose, but drawing attention to such is within the purview of an editor. No, David's emphasis is on the lessons embedded within his night journey. We likely can relate to David's journey, like the 2006 film,* Night at the Museum *(based on Milan Trenc's 1993 children's book). But unlike Stiller's blockbuster film trilogy about episodes after dark, David is more concerned with the Trinity and what happens in the light.*

▼ ▼ ▼

When I was in college, my bills were about to shackle me, and I sought some type of job—any job really—to be able to continue with classes. Thankfully, the church next to campus hired me as a night janitor.

I learned to sweep and mop floors, dust the beautiful light-colored wood in the building, arrange chairs, and yes, even clean urinals and toilets. I arrived at the church late at night in darkness and began my work. It consisted of menial tasks—but for a college student it afforded some peace and quiet and, most important, a paycheck.

It wasn't long before the job's repetitive nature bored me. Loneliness nearly overwhelmed me, until I stumbled across a stash of old cassette tapes in a forgotten church nook. Imagine a night janitor sporting an old Walkman, puffy earphones, and pushing a broom with a duster in his back pocket.

The cassettes contained sermons preached at least a decade earlier. Some of the tape threads had stretched over time, which raised the pitch of the preachers' voices. This was before iPods and streaming music offered unlimited options, so I kept listening to pass the time. The cache included memorable teaching on the feeding of the five thousand, the rich young ruler, and the man born blind, among others. I learned about obscure Old Testament prophets and even more about famous biblical characters such as Moses and Daniel.

After I had listened to all the tapes, I revisited my favorites. One set was a simple, verse-by-verse recording of the King James Version. It sounded odd to me—like listening to an obscure Shakespearean play. The Psalms, however, sounded particularly rhythmic in that old tongue. I'm sure I wore out that particular cassette.

Sometimes that church became rather scary in the middle of the night. With all but a few of the lights off, I would notice something moving in the distance. My heart jumped more than once. "Is someone here? A break-in? Did I leave a door unlocked?" The church was bright and cheerful on

Sunday morning, but at 1:30 a.m. with the lights off, a church can seem downright haunted.

Occasionally I would investigate and discover the youth pastor had just returned from a trip with the teens, disheveled and homeless looking, smelling of pizza and Mountain Dew. One time it was the senior pastor who couldn't sleep, so he came in to work on his unfinished sermon. I nearly gave my bald-headed, rosy-cheeked boss a heart attack when I came around the corner. After gasping, he paused for a kind conversation and even prayed with me for a moment.

Usually a "scare" revealed nothing unusual. I wondered if I had been imagining things or if there really were intruders hiding in the closets. In time, I came to think of the potential spook as the presence of something more supernatural, a sign that God was with me. I could sense his transforming presence right around the corner, watching me mop floors and clean toilets. I think back and wonder if the way I saw it was perhaps a bit shallow, maybe even superstitious. Or, maybe I was on to something.

Occasionally after phantom sightings, I would enter the large sanctuary, which was dark with only the streaks of moonlight shining down from the expansive 1960s glass-block windows on the left side. I would approach the cross at the front of the room and sometimes kneel and pray in my janitor clothes, remembering a similar trip during childhood.

At that very church, when I was just six years old, I had walked down the aisle to that same altar and knelt before that cross to receive Christ. This church had what many considered a bizarre layout. The prominent cross, crafted from the same light hardwood found throughout the church, was mounted in front of the platform, freestanding on the platform's stage just beyond the altar. That cross was sort of "in the way" of everything, which was both weird and wonderful. It seemed mammoth, around ten feet high and of substantial heft. Now as a night janitor, I knelt anew on that same carpet, faded if not frayed; the very steps I was about to vacuum.

After becoming a minister, I left the janitorial duties to others. I eventually returned to join the pastoral staff of that same church. (After all, I was rather familiar with its clean toilets and dust-free windows.) In time, we razed that old building and built a beautiful new one with dark wood and stained-glass windows. A brick from that old church remains on my shelf. Later on, I hired a night janitor for the new facility, remembering my own long nights with the broom and brushes, and my old friends—those worn tapes.

I have worked in a variety of roles in the church since then, and when I think about it, they are not all that different from my old nightly janitorial duties. At times my work is boring and repetitive. Sometimes even lonely. It still involves what amounts to cleaning up after other people and then getting everyone and everything ready for worship.

Most of all, it involves looking for God's transforming presence, even in the dark and lonely places—especially in the dark and lonely places. He is present, even now, if we would just look for him and kneel.

WHEN YOUR MOM FINALLY HUGS YOU

LEANN MARTENS

Editor's Note: *This story struck me more than any in the book. I first read it while sitting on the McDonald's patio near the Women's Bridge in Buenos Aires where all the streets leading to the bridge are named after women. In the case of the story below, we learn of many events in Leann's life that led her to a bridge to freedom—personal peace with who she is and what she fears. One of those is the fear of rejection or, at the least, distance from her mother. While I'll never forget the patio among Argentina's docks—it touched my soul in its own way—this story which I read there particularly moved me because I found myself in awe of a friend's fortitude, her strength in a private journey. I say private, because I know Leann; for a few summers we often golfed together during college outings. Until this story, I was unaware of any physical struggle, and certainly of any hint of timidity or rejection. She has always exhibited an admirable toughness, oftentimes the only woman among twenty to thirty men. On one legendary night, a young collegian shanked his drive from the second tee, and Leann, approaching the adjacent third green, took a direct hit to her shoulder. A few inches higher, and it could have killed her. Most other golfers would have gone back to the clubhouse. Not Leann. She finished the scramble event sporting a dark bruise the size of a Frisbee. Here she gives us insight on taking direct hits, so to speak, with unfortunate* *prognoses and continuing a pursuit of both goals and healing. We all need hugs!*

▼ ▼ ▼

A few years ago, I was diagnosed with scleroderma, an autoimmune disease that causes thickening of the skin. It can affect internal organs and I have lost 50 percent of my lung function. The journey has been difficult, but God has provided great doctors, medical care, and people who have supported me and prayed for me and my family. Many have prayed for physical healing, and although that has not happened, God has provided healing in other aspects of my life.

In September 2014, my birthday fast approaching, I flippantly told my daughter that I wanted to do a zip-line course, an activity that's rather out of character for me. For starters, I'm afraid of heights. She quickly replied, "Yes, we are going to do it!" Several years earlier, when our middle son was around nine, he wanted me to climb a fire tower with him. I was so frightened that I almost had a panic attack even thinking about the daunting cascade of steps. He kept encouraging me to accompany him, and I gave in. By focusing on the back of his tennis shoes, I made it to the top, one painful, frightening step at a time.

So, on a lovely fall day, I went with my daughter and a friend to a zip-line course. I am glad I didn't know what I was getting into. I had imagined one long zip line and wondered why it cost so much. Actually, the course included eight zip lines and four hanging bridges. When I stepped on the platform for the first zip line, I felt no fear, no racing heart, no stomach tension, and no panic. Most of my life I had felt all of those.

As I approached each new element of the course, I whispered, "I can do this," and proceeded. Perhaps that sounds simple to you. For me, however, it was anything but normal. Rather, for most of my life I had focused on fearful thoughts instead of realizing the truth: I actually could and can do it.

The last zip line stretched one thousand feet long. Most of it was over water, and we would be traveling about forty miles per hour. Did I mention that we were starting out eighty feet in the air? As I flew down the line, I joyously screamed, "I did it, yes!" But I celebrated a bit too soon and didn't make it all the way to the shore. Typically, if that happens, you turn around and do a hand-over-hand action to get to your destination. But after nearly three hours, my arms were like rubber and had no remaining strength. I could not even grip the cable. As a result, I slid on the cable farther away from the shore. I was hanging by a cable, suspended half in the water. At that moment, I experienced a peace I have rarely known. God was holding me in my utter weakness, and I could do nothing to help myself. That scene will forever be in my mind. God used a zip-line course to show me how much he had healed my age-old fears. He gave me his peace even in weakness and illness.

I am convinced that had I not attempted the zip-line course, I would not have been able to take on the challenge I faced a few months later.

My mom and I always had an OK relationship. She viewed it as really good, but I felt I could never connect with her emotionally. While I was growing up we didn't know how to talk about emotions, so I learned to turn them off and hide them away. I saw her as strong and capable of doing anything and she felt I was weak if I expressed emotions.

Through counseling I have worked on various issues, including my interactions with and response to Mom. Despite all of the work, I remained fearful of talking to her face-to-face about our relationship, past and present.

In October 2014, Mom was coming for a visit, an event I usually dread. I felt pressure to clean the house and have everything "together" before she arrived. I often scheduled brief times to escape from her. Talking about the upcoming visit, my husband commented that my family rarely talks directly to each other but rather about each other. The Holy Spirit then nudged me: I had never talked directly to Mom about my issues. So I boldly asked Mom to come to a counseling session with me. Surprisingly, she agreed.

At the session, I explained that this wasn't about blaming her for being a bad mother. The truth is, she had done some things really well and others not so well. (The same is true for me as a mother.) I asked her to listen and not say anything until I finished. Through counseling and many loving people in my life, I have learned to express my emotions and talk about situations. I wanted to do this with Mom, though I knew the session would be difficult—similar to attempting the zip-line course.

I started telling Mom about some difficult childhood experiences. After only a few sentences, Mom reached over and hugged me and began crying. One thing you need to know is that my family was not affectionate. We hugged only for hellos and goodbyes. Second, I had seen my strong mother cry only at funerals and here she was crying with me. I talked at length as my mom sat close and held my hand. Never in my life had I experienced her touch and comfort so tangibly, a connection so new, yet so good. My counselor said he had never seen an eighty-three-year-old woman respond in such an out-of-character way. It truly was a moment of God doing "immeasurably more than all we ask or imagine, according to his power that is at work within us" (Eph. 3:20).

We spent the next few days covering new territory: discussing family issues and relationships. Here, God was doing his healing work. He was answering the prayers of many in a different way than any of us expected.

So often it is easy to think of something we want to do. At times we sense the Holy Spirit compelling us toward a specific action or direction, but fear prevents us from taking those steps. Acknowledging our fears and taking those steps of faith, however large or small, is crucial. It is in those zip-line moments, amid those steps of faith that take us into places we feared to go, that God reveals he is strong even in our weakness. God can use these lessons revealing his grace and love to heal us and restore our most tender relationships.

RADICAL HOPE

JOHN McCRACKEN

Editor's Note: *Each Sunday across the pews I see friends from a variety of professions. Beauticians, janitors, wealth investors, artists, carpenters, teachers, and those representing a host of other specialties. It's part of the joy of community. When you worship together long enough, it's easy to be in awe of others' gifts in areas foreign to your own, and you enjoy their company no matter what.*

Dr. John McCracken is such a person. Sometimes everyone at the table or coffee discussion has different skills, and I often see him in groups encompassing a mélange of interests and talents. When among them, John reminds me of the beauty of the Romans 12 passage—the value of different members of the same body. John McCracken is one of those group members possessing intriguing gifts and interests. He has long established himself as a master teacher and storyteller. He's eloquent with phrases, whether in his own written work or as he's relaying another's. And he doesn't publicly cite a book or story that's not to be taken seriously.

John is that tall, well-dressed man you see in a crowd and wonder what part of the world he's from and what adventures he's had. And you're likely curious about where he's just returned from. Whether in a wool vest or a Lands' End shirt, he embodies that professional protocol for teachers that expects attire befitting of the calling. And for Dr. McCracken, there is no higher calling than teaching literature and being a provocateur through creative writing.

The following submission begins appropriately with an interaction with one of his friends. Oh, Emily Dickinson has been dead for around 120 years, but, knowing John, I immediately assumed the line was from this Amherst recluse. John's stature and brilliance remind me of the author-pastor John Ortberg, who helped a group of us pioneer a church in California. It's hard not to smile when you see either John; everyone seems to enjoy their time with them. But in light of the above, keep in mind that the following poem is far from glib verse. I know just enough of Dr. McCracken's journey to know that his faith needs a firmly held hope, more deeply rooted than the ephemeral types. As poems often do, this one prompts us to think through what's behind it, and reflect on where and how it intersects with our own journeys.

▼   ▼   ▼

Emily once said
that "hope is the thing with feathers
that perches in the soul,"[1]
But I have no need
for a hope like
a "thing with feathers."
Its hollow bones snap at the slightest pressure;
so easily crushed in the world's rough fist.

I need durable, sturdy, resilient hope;
a rock congealed in the forges of earth:
diamond hard,
enduring,

indestructible.
A sixties radical hope
that stands up to protest injustice
then suffers the dogs and water cannons of oppression
and stands up again.

I don't need hope to "perch in my soul";
precariously situated so the slightest
wind can sweep it away.

I need a radical hope
that inhabits my entire soul
and puts down deep roots
no gale could displace.
Radical hope
is not the kind that nests in the spring
and is gone in the winter;
migratory, based on how the wind blows.
It's not a downy comfort
to warm our frosty hearts
in time of darkness.

Radical hope
is a cornerstone
bought with the blood of the Holy One;
a strong tower in time of need,
a staging site from which I participate
in his occupations,
a real reason for living.

Radical hope is the thing with teeth
that bites into the soul and will not let go.

NOTE

1. Emily Dickinson, "'Hope' Is the Thing with Feathers," in *The Poems of Emily Dickinson,* ed. R. W. Franklin (Cambridge, MA: Harvard University Press, 1999), no. 314.

SOUL SHIFT TAKES TIME

BUTCH SEARS

Editor's Note: *I love running into Butch at church. He's a polite but tenacious version of George Carlin in suspenders. We became acquainted through Sunday school and then talks in the church hallways; his voice tone, smile, and intensity are curiously magnetic. At times he seems frail, with a gingerly walk, and at other times remarkably strong. From a distance he looks like a bearded exclamation mark. Over the years, I've noticed that Butch is among the most consistent volunteers to help with projects around the church or to help the disenfranchised. His name often surfaces when I follow up with my wife about her day at the church office. She mentions his help or his comments on one of my articles, or I see him when I pick her up for lunch. He seems like the perpetual volunteer.*

Though at times his Walt Whitman earthiness might conjure one assumed profile, when I visited his home a while back I saw one of the most organized garages in town. From pristine classics, to motorcycles and tool arrangements, Butch has an industrious side. I think he's retired, but he always seems to be working, even after serious heart issues. We stood in his garage next to his old gray Chevy and talked about a project he was helping a shut-in with. Through the years he had never mentioned his man cave, cars, and service to the disenfranchised. He's not the type you'll see quoted on the news. His name isn't in the headlines. He doesn't sing in church, and I don't think he teaches or preaches. But he's got his niche and a network of people and programs that depend on him—and what nobler role could one hope for? At his home, I got the sense that he is one of the mainstays of his neighborhood, among the type of men I remember visiting often in different places I've lived— people I just liked spending time with. Young men need folk like Butch.

▼   ▼   ▼

Some idioms can be haunting, like, "That apple didn't fall far from the tree." So people like me are left to ask, are all apples from my family tree rotten? And it can nag at you when things go sour, making you wonder if whole orchards in a family line are tainted. Somehow destined for destruction.

Perhaps I'm in that sunset of life that President Reagan once mentioned. If so, I'm struck with my own life's metaphor. Regardless of what kind of apple I was when Jesus picked me up, it's what I have become that counts. What if I had asked Jesus to make me his much earlier in my life?

In retrospect, reflecting on my life and earlier generations, I've learned that what once seemed so normal was replete with sin. The daily routines I experienced led to a sinful normalcy in my life and in the lives of others. For generations many in my family made this mistake, accepting unproductive and often destructive habits. My story is still being written, and some pages need to be torn out still. However, I'm here to tell you that, thanks be to God, my soul is shifting. It may have taken a few more decades than it could have, but what's happening now inside me has currency—eternity.

My life is really a tale of two stories. The first is fraught with anger at a background filled with family traditions and sordid scenarios. My ancestry had, by many accounts, put me in a position doomed from the beginning. I realize now that traditions should be about passing down the best of practices to the next generation. But when a family's gauge of "best" is skewed, so are traditions. My anger has softened recently, as I've come to accept that my elders were probably, without much thought, modeling traditions handed to them. History was not a good teacher for me, and it's taken me too many decades to become a good pupil. That's changed.

The second story shares some pages with the first, but the theme is different. It's a story focused on the present, not the past, concentrating on a shift in my soul. It's definitely a story in the present tense, and its conclusion is uncertain—but I'm really trying. I knew that committing to the shift, although scary, was the only way to find peace in a life now adorned with gray hair and grandkids. The short of it: sixty years of pain is way too many. I'm more of a talker than a writer, but, if I were to write this second story, I think my life is still in chapter 1. Relapses to some characteristics of my old self still occur, but they are much less frequent. And as I'm outlining the sections of this second story, chapter 2 would be titled "Hope."

But looking forward, my hope is that chapter 2 will help others find peace in their own stories and realize that they are not alone. I thank College Wesleyan Church for its patience and for introducing me to a life that gives hope through Christ.

Perhaps the need to feel included is quintessentially human and it's something with which I still struggle. Being included often appears elusive for me. Whether it's being surrounded by folk with doctorates, talking to those from many generations of tight Christian families, or simply noting the divide between my family and those of wealth, I think too often about whether I fit in. I'm pretty sure this is a lingering disposition from my upbringing.

Through this journey, however, I've strongly felt God's presence—especially during the past three years. The focus and clear lessons of the book, *SoulShift*, have been instrumental in this growth. This book, written by our pastors, Steve DeNeff and David Drury, fosters spiritual transformation and was the center of our church life for several weeks. We walked through it chapter by chapter, one per week.[1] God has helped me to identify the source of my pain, and I've been addressing it. Through the *SoulShift* project and other endeavors, God has helped me to understand the church's mission.

SoulShift training and its corresponding sermons were, and are, transforming my spiritual life. Have you ever had a season in which life just seemed to look different? That's where I'm at as I write this. It's a journey, and my life is still changing; for a wonderfully pleasant stretch, I've not had lingering relapses to my old self.

God is indeed patient. When negative thoughts seep into my mind, he reminds me of his promises. We often talk into the night, which frequently involves long reflections on this journey called life. During these sessions God helps me realize the striking difference between his divine plan, which includes both the local and universal church, and the rampant and destructive tendencies of the world. And—this is the kicker—he shows me that I don't have to worry as much about those worldly tendencies, as my home is much different now that God is in control of my life. And he shows me that my wife and I have control over our own home. For me, it's also over my garage, where I spend much time. God lets me know during tough spells that we're going to get past this—that it might be dark but keep in mind, "It's Friday, but Sunday's coming." There is indeed hope.

One overriding lesson from these past few years is that soul shift, at least for me, takes time. I can chart my life story nicely into chapters, and I think it's helpful for a lot of people to do the same for their lives. But in the end, my own story's chapters sure take a lot longer to live than reading the book that's helping me to shape and edit them. And I'm learning that that's OK.

NOTE

1. Steve DeNeff and David Drury, *SoulShift: The Measure of a Life Transformed* (Wesleyan Publishing House, 2011). More than a thousand other churches have used this book and its corresponding resources.

HE MAKES ALL THINGS NEW

MARILYN M. SMITH

Editor's Note: Many of us can point to a pivotal year in which key events, people, illnesses, blessings, or some other assortment of the unusual, changed the landscape of our lives. For Marilyn M. Smith, that pivotal event was an unwelcome divorce. While it seems as if such a major transition would always be a watershed, too often it's not. Below we find a transparency about how God worked in her life and continues to use and shape her. Throughout this process, as she illustrates, we also see that part of a pivotal moment is coming to terms with our humanness and need for God's touch.

The pivotal year of my life was 1983. On the downside, I endured a painful divorce. But the upside was eternally transformative: I was born again. The ending of any marriage shouldn't be blissful, and mine was no exception. Rather, it was a reality that cut deep into my soul, deeper than I realized at the time. But simultaneously a newly acquired joy through Christ brought a sustaining hope.

A spirit of rejection overwhelmed me leading into, during, and after the divorce. At the time, I was unaware of the source of my feelings and reactions. In retrospect, I realize that my paranoia, especially in my response to others' comments, was tied to this spirit of rejection. I regularly misconstrued others' remarks and often thought that most people were against me. The spirit of rejection is like a weed that spreads and grows. In my experience, this spirit has twin companions—fear and offense.

The change for the better began later in 1983. I was sound asleep one Saturday night when a booming voice awakened me. It declared, "And be not conformed to this world: but be ye transformed by the renewing of your mind, that ye may prove what is that good, and acceptable, and perfect, will of God" (Rom. 12:2 KJV). The voice was so big and powerful it seemed to push me back down in the bed; my whole body trembled. Those words were new to me as a new believer; I had only recently started reading my Bible.

During church the next morning, I began to understand more fully what had transpired. As the pastor began to preach from the same passage—Romans 12—the lights went on. God had roused my attention with that thunderous voice in the middle of the night. This may seem overly simplified. Fantastic. Miraculous. All that I know is what I heard and its effect: the abrupt ending to any sense of loneliness. Whenever God speaks to humans, it's the supernatural interacting with the natural. Yes, that's a miracle.

God's call on my life became abundantly and immediately clear. I was to devote my talents and resources to the ministry of evangelism. God opened many doors in the months that followed. After ministry engagements in northern Indiana, my home state, offers came from other states and countries. Through these efforts, bathed in much prayer, God was working in a wide array of people. Some came to him for salvation, others to be filled with the Holy Spirit, and many others for healing and various other types of divine help. Only God knows the fullness of his work, but he allowed me a glimpse of his outpouring.

The irony is that I still needed help overcoming the spirit of rejection. Our personal crises, such as divorce, can exacerbate issues that run deep and long into the future. Finally, God was helping me through this. I've also learned that hindsight isn't always 20/20; why hadn't I seen my shortcomings earlier and understood why I became irritated and even offensive?

God stepped in and helped me break this cycle. Once again I heard him loud and clear. This time he was going to remove my "heart of stone" and replace it with a "heart of flesh" with the capacity to love and forgive (see Ezek. 36:26). To empathize. To give with no sense of expectation of receiving something in return. And, most important, a heart focused on God and others and not myself. "Woe is me" would become an idiom and not a personal maxim.

Another pivotal event was fulfilling the request to deliver the eulogy at my sister's funeral. Amidst their sadness and aching hearts, some relatives were hurtful to others, including me. God reminded me that he was making all things new, including my heart. The spirit of service and love had supplanted that of rejection. Passages like Exodus 14:13 brought comfort. It reads, "See the salvation of the LORD, which he will work for you today. For the Egyptians whom you see today, you shall never see again" (ESV).

Despite all that was happening around me, I no longer reacted in anger and resentment; rather, I saw the manifestation of the fruit of the Spirit in me: love, joy, peace, patience, kindness, goodness, faithfulness, gentleness, and self-control. With such a bumper crop of fruit, there wasn't any room for rejection or resentment. The weeds of fear and offense had no room to take root. I didn't feel any hurt or anger. The feeling of rejection was gone!

The basis of the eulogy was 1 Corinthians 13, God's agape love and his call for us to love each other. God moved in our presence, healing our wounds. Where hours earlier hurt and tension existed, miraculously peace abounded.

Perhaps it's true for all of us that we never feel like a finished product but one in process. God is making me new by transforming my mind and the growth continues. The pivotal year of 1983 showed me glimpses of the best and worst of life: the harshness of earthly entanglements and the contrasting refreshment of heavenly interruptions. From my vantage point more than thirty years later, I can look back through my journey's window and see clearly that God has delivered me. And, though it's not funny, I can only chuckle that it took me so many years. But that chuckle is enveloped in a widespread joy. Knowing that God continues his transforming work in me, I'm walking in freedom.

JOY THAT OVERFLOWS
PRAYER SURE CAN CHANGE A PERSON

ALICE WILLS

Editor's Note: Perhaps every church has a member who exudes confidence in 150-point font, bold and underlined. For me, that's Alice Wills. She was the head librarian and kept all operations in perfect shape at the old Goodman Library, now transformed into the building that houses my office. Her parents were fixtures around campus during my student days, along with her late husband, Gordon, pleasantly active until the day of his unexpected passing. Alice, like her mother, has never been successful as a whisperer (ironic, considering she was a librarian). The energy in her conversations seems linked to her volume button—which I find delightful. Though I've enjoyed her for several decades, her chapter below caused me to pause and realize anew the silent journey of many of the saints in our midst. From my current perspective, I wonder if I could have reminded her occasionally how she's such a beautiful addition to my own journey, a consistent figure whose energy is appreciated. But her transparency here is as refreshing as my recollection of her presence. She really challenges us to create time and space for those with whom we worship with—to find moments and places that allow them to tell their stories, to grow, to be loved, and love freely. I've always felt she has done the latter well, but from her statements, perhaps her love and attendant joy came midway through her journey.

➤ ➤ ➤

I have been a Christian for as long as I can remember. I have always wanted to serve the Lord and do what is right, but I knew I didn't have the power to do it. I have always had an inferiority complex and never liked myself. I resented the Lord for making me the way I was and for making my parents the way they were because I could see their bad traits in myself.

These weren't my only resentments. I resented pretty women—because I wasn't pretty. I resented calm, composed, quiet women—because I lacked those qualities. I looked scornfully at people who dressed extremely modestly; who did they think they were, being so spiritual? And people who dressed immodestly; how could they profess to be Christians?

I liked my work as a librarian and would have found it difficult to quit. Yet I begrudged having to work full-time, raise three girls, and be a pastor's wife. I came home at the end of the day so tired I couldn't go pastoral calling with my husband. Actually, I was glad I couldn't go, because I didn't like visiting homes. In fact, I didn't like people very well—at all.

For years I got up early to have devotions. At first, I admit, my motivation was questionable—I was tired of feeling guilty under conviction for neglecting the practice. Then eventually I enjoyed the quiet time, which made me feel righteous, countering my inner restlessness. But I still needed more from the Lord. I was unpleasant around my family and wanted them to appreciate what I did for them. They didn't seem to change and deep down in my heart I knew I was at fault.

I read Isaiah 44:3 over and over again: "For I will pour water on the thirsty land, and streams on the dry ground; I will pour out my Spirit on your offspring, and my blessing on your descendants."

Mostly I wanted to claim the last part for my girls' salvation. But the first part kept impressing me. I was thirsty. "Lord, pour water on me!" I'd ask. Yet God seemed to ignore my prayers and I just accepted reality as I saw it: I would never be happy.

One day I prayed, "Make me easier to live with and I'll be satisfied not being happy." But that prayer, too, seemed to be ignored.

I had been reading *Absolute Surrender* by Andrew Murray. Some sections spoke to my heart and piqued my awareness of spiritual possibilities. Other sections I didn't like at all; I knew the experience he described was not for me.

By this time, I had reached the end of myself. One evening, I went to my bedroom, picked up Murray's book, and read a selection about righteous activity. "Been there, done that," I thought. But I kept reading about the Holy Spirit trying to get into a heart but only being able to seep in and around all the other things. I laid down the book and felt compelled to pour out all my resentments through prayer. I confessed my worthless righteous activity: "Lord, I don't care if you don't do anything for me. I just want to get all this negativity out of my heart." When I got through confessing, I felt empty. I had nothing to stand on. "Lord, have mercy," I cried.

Then I quoted and claimed 1 John 1:9 for myself: "If we confess our sins, he is faithful and just and will forgive us our sins and purify us from all unrighteousness." Suddenly my thoughts changed in realization: "I'm different, I love everybody. My resentments are gone, and I feel free and clean." I even looked down at myself to see if it was still me!

The next day, I looked through Murray's book to read those good words again, but they weren't there! The Lord had put those words in that book when I needed them.

I learned some lessons from that experience. I know that the Lord can change a person and yet leave him or her as essentially the same person. I know that outward circumstances do not need to change or spoil inner peace and happiness. It's only my attitude that can spoil them. I need only concern myself with what I do. Other people's actions aren't my concern.

My attitude changed my family, my marriage, and the church. I asked for drops of mercy and I received showers of blessings. I pray that others will come to the water and experience the joy.

PART 5

THE TRUTH OF GOD'S PROVIDENCE

STRANGER IN THE WHITE HOUSE

JEFF CLARK

Editor's Note: Some couples have a magnetic presence. It's just fun to bump into them in town, or anticipate gatherings where your paths intersect. That's the Clarks. Young. Vibrant. Hoosier classy—which means hospitable, down to earth, and lovers of basketball. One place you'll always find them is at the Indiana Wesleyan University men's basketball games, where Jeff serves as the assistant coach. Don't let assistant *mislead you; there's a mind-set among that staff that it's truly a team. It's been obvious to many that Jeff could have accepted head coaching jobs elsewhere—especially after winning the national championship. The head coach has also turned down offers—it's assumed that's because of the special friendship and mission connection with Jeff and other colleagues. The following story about Jeff mentoring his son, Josh, gives you a glimpse of the passion Jeff has for the players. It's not just about putting the ball through the rim, but facilitating the players through their goals and to eternal gates. A few guests to the campus have commented that the highlight of their visits was attending a session in the locker room with Jeff and his colleagues. Considering he works at a campus replete with stunning buildings and vibrant programs, that's quite a compliment.*

▼ ▼ ▼

Some moments with children begin as attempts to teach them, but soon the adults become the students. That's what transpired the day our son, Josh, almost three years old at the time, pointed to a stranger's house, indicating we should visit and invite them to pray.

The scenario started when I listened to a radio interview in which a pastor cautioned that parents focus too much on providing information about God rather than modeling and introducing meaningful ways to experience God. At the college, we call this experiential learning, *praxis*: an approach to teaching and learning with proven results, often with life-changing outcomes. God convicted me that I had not applied this well-known dynamic with my fathering.

The pastor's simple message was profound: if parents disciple their children in ways that involve practical and tangible outcomes, their excitement for their faith will more likely endure. My hope is for a life-long faith, an eternal faith.

As I prayed for direction on practical ways to test this out, an idea immediately came to mind. I rushed home and loaded Josh into the car, and yes, with the cautious approval of my supportive but unconvinced wife, I asked Josh to pray that we would experience God together and that God would show us a way to encourage a family that needed a boost. I gave Josh permission to direct me anywhere he felt led in Marion: "Let me know when you see a house you want to pray for." Before long we were knocking on the door of a family we had never met.

"I have been teaching my son about prayer and as we were driving by he mentioned he wanted to pray for your family. Do you have any specific prayer needs, and would you be willing to allow my son to pray for you?"

I'm not sure what I expected in this "faith lesson" for Josh, but the uneventful response from the homeowner disappointed me. The person said, "We regularly attend a local church; we would love prayer." I should have been elated with their receptivity, and I should have been even more excited when Josh prayed aloud for these strangers, but I had hoped for something "greater" from this fathering experiment.

The larger context is that I had recently had a nagging fear about Josh's future love of Jesus. I was overwhelmed by the statistics that showed the number of young people who walk away from the Lord when they move away from their supportive Christian surroundings. My fear for his future adversely affected my faith in God's plan.

As he does so often, the Spirit spoke a well-timed truth into my life. As I loaded Josh back into the car, I complimented him: "Now, let's go tell your mom about how you prayed so well. You weren't afraid to pray with a stranger." And, you likely guessed it, here's where I became the pupil.

"No, Daddy, we can't go home," he replied. "There is another family we need to pray for."

My curiosity was piqued. "OK, which direction should we go in?"

After he guided me to make a couple of turns, he identified a house. We were not in the most reputable part of town, and I instinctively chose the nicer of the two homes he could have been pointing to.

"No, Daddy," said Josh, "we need to pray for the people at the white house."

That particular house manifested all the stereotypical aspects I had imagined for a scary house, or at least one our son should avoid. Mud now stood where the sidewalk used to be. Only three of the six windows facing the road were completely covered with glass, and the screen door did not shut.

Deep down, I knew that avoiding this house would go against the point of this experiment, so I reluctantly knocked on the door. A young mother answered. When she opened the door, I saw her two preschoolers, one about Josh's age, and a young man—her boyfriend—who at first kept his distance.

As we talked, we adults discovered a connection to a mutual friend in town. Josh found some common ground with the child, and before we left

Josh prayed for the family. Walking back to the car, I felt a peace from God that Josh was in God's hands.

Before we even arrived at home, I received a phone call from the mutual friend. He'd already heard about our visit. "I've been witnessing to them for months," he explained, "and then you knock on their door!" The young woman had been wanting to accept this friend's invitation to attend his family's church, but the boyfriend had been skeptical. As it turned out, as soon as Josh left his house, the young man turned to his girlfriend and said that if God could speak through a two-year-old, they should probably give the church a try.

My wife and I have thought back on this experience often, as we've been blessed with two more sons. It has motivated us to pray aggressively for them, that they would not just be men who know about God, but they would know God personally, and have life experiences on which they could hang a lifetime of questions and answers.

While we hope that they know a lot about God, we want them to know that the kingdom of God is not a matter of talk, but of power! It has motivated us to take the ceiling off of what God can do through them, even at their young age, if they fearlessly follow him. In turn, it has sparked us to desire this same fearless mentality in our own relationship with the Father.

IN GOD'S PERFECT TIME

CAROL BENCE

Editor's Note: *Some couples are smart, their kids are smart, and likely even their dog is smart. That's the Bud and Carol Bence family. All three of their children are now professionals. Bud, a theology professor, is known nationally for his preaching. Carol established herself as a leader among the nursing community, where she was the fulcrum of much growth at Indiana Wesleyan University, and whatever she wears, her social etiquette, even her diction, is categorically flawless. People love Carol as the paragon of politeness with class. While Bud is smart, he's not gifted in the same ways. Shirt usually untucked on one side, hands flailing all over as he talks, and coffee mugs left in a zillion places around campus where he forgot them—people love him for his explosive charisma and recognize his powerful presence. The whole Bence family is indeed special.*

This is a story focused on their daughter Aimee. I was privileged to have her in the first group of the JCBodyshop, the youth program attached to College Wesleyan Church. It seems that any high school coach or youth pastor remains those students' youth pastor or coach for the rest of their lives. For years now, I've been introduced as such to Aimee's friends. She was gifted in both sports and studies in high school, and she's simply a gift wherever she's planted.

▼　▼　▼

Our daughter Aimee spent much of her early-adult life building her career as a medicinal chemist and has had a fulfilling job at Eli Lilly Pharmaceuticals in Indianapolis. Every Saturday night a group of young Lilly professionals would meet at a Mexican restaurant south of the city for congeniality and friendship. There, Aimee got to know a young colleague, Burch, and one evening he asked Aimee out to dinner—just a casual evening. Over dinner, Burch spent a good deal of time talking about how he valued being young and single. Burch had a very sharp mind, evident in the invigorating conversation that appealed to Aimee.

As dinners piled on top of dinners, the friendship became deeper and turned into love for both of them. However, Aimee had spiritual concerns. Burch had come from a secular and culturally Buddhist background. Although he had many Christian friends and influences, he noted that they often seemed uncomfortable with his difficult faith-related questions and Burch frequently found their dogmatic answers less than satisfying. Aimee had a strong belief in Jesus Christ, but she herself had unanswered questions. As they both talked openly, many hours of conversation ensued, often centered on the ideas of C. S. Lewis and his path of faith.

Aimee offered Burch a Bible and suggested he read the gospel of Mark. But, thinking it strange to begin in the middle of a book, he went straight to Genesis. He asked Aimee and us many questions, such as why a loving God would ask Abraham to kill his son, Isaac. As Aimee and Burch studied the Bible together, Aimee explained how she had wrestled with her own faith issues and reconciled them as she found truth. Aimee's father, Bud, and Burch periodically engaged in serious inquiry. Once Burch asked Bud, "In the Christian life, how does one know when enough is enough?"—citing the story of the rich young ruler (see Matt. 19:16–30). And also, "What do you do with a God who changes from the

Old Testament to the New Testament when it is thought that God is the same, yesterday, today, and forever?" Burch later said he was captivated with Bud, a seasoned theologian who also grappled with faith questions. Burch had observed so many Christians who accepted so much about their faith without questioning.

I remember a Sunday at College Wesleyan Church when Aimee and Burch came to church with us. Being Easter morning, the white cloth draped the empty cross. The cloth was slowly moving, possibly from air currents blowing across the chancel. To me it was symbolic evidence of the Holy Spirit moving in Burch's life. That spring morning, I prayed fervently for Burch to find the path to Christ.

Family and friends also joined us in praying for Burch and Aimee. Burch told us he could not become a Christian just so he could marry Aimee, and we greatly respected him for his honesty. We grew to love Burch, a genuine person of integrity who enriched and challenged Aimee in every way.

As love deepened between Aimee and Burch, they talked of marriage. Aimee wrestled with marrying someone who was not a professing believer. We also, as her parents, cried out to God on their behalf. The day came when Burch asked Bud for our consent to the marriage, including a request for Bud to perform the ceremony. How should an ordained minister in The Wesleyan Church respond to that request?

We sought direction from God and from strong faith-full friends. After much prayer and fasting, we gave our blessing to the marriage. We did not want to lose a daughter or a future son-in-law to the faith and to the family, should we erect barriers. Not all of our family supported us in this decision, which was painful at times, but we believed God was leading us in this decision.

By the time of their engagement, Burch was attending Aimee's evangelical church and was moving along the path of faith. Both Aimee and

Burch's desire for a church wedding became problematic when several churches refused to open their doors to a wedding between a Christian and a non-Christian. But Aimee and Burch were married on August 10, 2012, in a Wesleyan church in Indianapolis, with Bud officiating. We asked a young artist friend, Evan Mazellan, to paint a triptych as a bridal gift, depicting the paths of the faith journey. Once prominent among early Christians, these three-paneled paintings remain common among various strands of faith. Bud focused his homily on the three images. The themes seemed to resonate with Burch's family, and they said it was a lovely ceremony.

Many Christians view their faith as a series of landmark events. But Burch has viewed his acceptance of things of faith as a journey; while significant waypoints might be marked, the path to faith itself was a seamless continuum that started long before "coming to faith." We continued to pray earnestly that Burch would travel this path of faith and that one of his waypoints would be to come to know the living God. Many faith conversations ensued between Aimee and Burch and our family. Burch's most insightful spiritual questions helped Bud and me clarify and enrich our faith in new ways.

In time, the Lord sparked new insights for Burch. In Indianapolis, he volunteered every week coaching with Special Olympics. At the gym, he noticed the way a fellow volunteer, named Tyler, related to the team players. Then he discovered that Tyler was an assistant pastor at Traders Point Christian Church, which he and Aimee attended. He wrote to us, "It may be mere coincidence that I meet Tyler at Special Olympics then meet him again at Traders Point, or it may be part of a larger plan. I'm warming up to the 'larger plan' perspective." Burch was moving down the path of faith.

Several months later, the day before Thanksgiving, Burch sent Bud an email: "I have decided to be baptized into the community of our Lord." Few moments will be etched in my mind quite like that one, as Bud and

I both wept at God's abundant mercy in opening Burch's heart and mind to the power of the living God. That season was truly a time of Thanksgiving. The Lord had heard our prayers.

Burch was baptized at Traders Point Christian Church the following February. Two pews of family and friends shared that joyous experience. Some of Burch's Purdue classmates who had shared the gospel with him from as far back as eighth grade sat with us. Later, Burch wrote to us, "Thanks for bringing Aimee into the world as she is such a joy. And thanks for being so wonderfully supportive in my journey to Christ." Although Burch viewed this step as a significant one on his path of faith, it was not the endpoint, but rather a gate to step through. Rather than having the gate in front of him, it was now behind him. The path of faith extends beyond baptism and continues on, as not all of the questions and doubts go away. Burch's view of the Christian life as a path *of* faith, rather than a path *to* faith, is a challenging perspective to Aimee as he continues on his journey.

Bud and I, too, learned many faith lessons. We desired to do the right thing, but sometimes it is very difficult to know what the right thing is in a given situation. Burch recently said to us, "You and your family's quiet, introspective representation of faith has helped me down the path tremendously." Bud and I tried to sense and follow God's leading in the darkness when we could not see in front of us. But we heard God's voice behind us saying, "This is the way; walk in it" (Isa. 30:21), and we did. It was a defining moment of trust as we walked into the light! Even today, Aimee and Burch continue to walk on their path of faith, which is as it should be in the Christian life. We rejoice that together they are on the path that leads to a life that lasts forever.

RENEWED IN MIND AND SPIRIT

RON MAZELLAN

Editor's Note: *Most churches have a list of people who are immediately recognized for their giftedness, from lawnmower repair, legal acuity, and cooking, to teaching, business, and singing. The list is long. At our particular church, which runs somewhere around fifteen hundred in attendance, we have an inordinate number of world-class artists. Not just "Oh, you're good!" but bestseller good! One of these is Ron, who shares a glimpse of his story below. It's not about his accomplishments, and not even about this talent or vocation. Rather, it's about one of his lessons from a personal shortcoming. That's Ron, a middle-aged man with a great family of strappingly handsome boys. His receding hairline betrays his age, but so does his social maturity. People love Ron, a pillar of the church and perpetually self-effacing.*

I recall the night when some of his peers wanted to celebrate his first bestselling book. We had a professional banner made: "Home of a New York Times Best Seller: Ron Mazellan." And I think we listed the title of that book as well (with coauthor Cal Ripkin Jr.; his next best seller was with Tony Dungy; and others won distinction, including from the NAACP). We snuck up to his yard on a busy street near downtown. His picturesque yellow Victorian home is the focal point as people drive up the hill. And there, as plain as anything, we firmly planted our wonderful banner. His car being parked at the back of the house, he likely wouldn't see the banner until he came home from work the next day. But, true to Ron's shyness, somehow he learned of the praise on display, and not long into the morning the banner was gone. That's Ron.

▼   ▼   ▼

Most people know me as an art professor and many locally seem to know me as "that artist guy." But there's that sports enthusiast within me that likely will never leave. Except for my undergraduate friends, most people don't know that I once played football. The closest association in their minds with Mazellans and sports is through my sons' impressive wrestling histories.

I love my art profession, but the football days remain such an important part of my life. Key life lessons stuck with me. I'm currently in the midst of a major illustrated book on NFL training camps, and the project brings these nostalgic moments back with more frequency.

Imagine my elation, then, when my old college coach, Dr. Cliff Schimmels, came to the campus where I work to speak in chapel. He's an extraordinary educator and it was such a privilege to play for him.

Nearly a decade had passed since we last talked, and the time gap only enhanced my excitement. My wife, Jil, and I would have the privilege of hosting him and his wife, Paula, during their brief stay in Marion. Anticipating our reunion, I recalled my student days at Wheaton College in Illinois, remembering especially Schimmels's unique teaching style, sincere mentoring, and commitment to coaching. An exhaustive list of defining memories returned with a flood of emotion, and I was eager to discuss the past, if the opportunity arose.

But Coach, in vintage Schimmels style, turned my plans into a penetrating teaching moment. One simple, yet defining, question shattered my long-held memories of the past.

As the four of us prepared to leave our home for campus, I turned to face him and, without much conscious thought, said, "Coach, do you remember the game—(referring to a grueling defeat)?"

He abruptly stopped walking, paused, and looked straight through me. His voice was kindhearted but direct as he considered his reply: "Ron Mazellan, is that all you remember?"

I felt strangely reprimanded by his question, as if I was being awakened from a deep, distant sleep. I was immediately saddened by my instant recall, though more shocked by the incongruity of his recollection and mine. My first stated memory seemed glazed with muted, dark tones. In contrast, his was bright, exuberant, and filled with memorable lessons of what we learned together in the classroom and on the football field. For me, our brief interaction set off a massive God-inspired paradigm shift.

I wanted to let go of his question, but I soon realized my negative automatic responses had already permeated countless memories. In response, I decided to predetermine my thoughts and actions with affirming outcomes. I began to saturate my mind with God's Word as it reflects the character of his Son and the hope he communicated.

As a matter of practice, I reflect on the good character of an individual, rather than the judgment of the person's flaws. In addition, I choose to retain hope and joy, rather than despair. Furthermore, I seek out what is succeeding in others and strive to pour inspiring influence into any critique of challenging situations. I admit I don't do this perfectly, as my wife will attest. My discipline of altering an automatic response is not the denial of heartbreaking experiences. The intent is to instill hope with a renewed tone regarding my journey and that of others in my community.

Nothing sets the perspective of my path in a more affirming direction than Philippians 4:8–9.

Summing it all up, friends, I'd say you'll do best by filling your minds and meditating on things true, noble, reputable, authentic, compelling, gracious—the best, not the worst; the beautiful, not the ugly; things to praise, not things to curse. Put into practice what you learned from me, what you heard and saw and realized. Do that, and God, who makes everything work together, will work you into his most excellent harmonies. (MSG)

FINDING GOD IN UNEXPECTED PLACES

GARY L. OTT

Editor's Note: When I drive north from Marion, Indiana, to golf, I enjoy passing the sprawling estate of Gary and Connie Ott. It's a taste of Kentucky horse farms and, at night, an unpainted Thomas Kinkaide scene. Endless white fences frame a picturesque manse that casts its shadow on a pond. The Otts' barns are nicer than most homes, and their helicopter worth more than some city blocks. They're obviously wealthy; in 2014 they donated money to expand a nursing and science facility at Indiana Wesleyan University (IWU). Although he's the founder of TLC Healthcare, he's not that far removed from unemployment and near financial ruin. He and his brothers now own or manage sixteen skilled nursing homes and several auxiliary companies, but there was a day Gary worried about having a home. Though he and his brothers also own another six assisted living facilities, he once needed assistance for survival. People like Gary don't turn many calendar pages before looking for next steps, for fresh opportunities to achieve and serve. During my college years at IWU, I lived in Ott House, a testimony of the generosity in Gary's heritage. It stood adjacent to where the stalwart Ott Hall of Sciences and Nursing stands today. Although I'm not a man of means, and most of whatever "success" I've had has been with words and not greenbacks, Gary's notion of "pivotal events" resonates with my journey, and perhaps with yours.

▼ ▼ ▼

Jobless, I became so despondent in 1987 that I just got in my car and drove randomly, eventually circling the Marion courthouse until I either ran out of gas or someone miraculously called me with job offer. In reality, I was desperate for God to take control of my life. Shortly after my arrival in Marion, newly hired to fly a corporate jet, my employer had gone belly up. Before long my stomach was in knots with worry about how to keep our kids' bellies full. Our whole family slept around the fireplace at night to keep warm.

I circled the courthouse after responding to yet another job opening posted in the paper. It sounded like an executive job with a vehicle provided. I put on my suit and, with résumé in-hand, went there, only to learn it was a carpet-cleaning job; the vehicle was a truck. There's nothing at all wrong with such a role, but prior to my move to Marion I had been an engineer for Texas Instruments and the work seemed too far removed from my calling.

A while before, when the original pilot job that brought me to Marion fell through, I had applied for a copilot position for Nationwide Management, a nursing home management company. But to qualify, they had said I'd have to get my nursing home administrator's license. Being completely disinterested in working in a nursing home, I had continued my job search.

Several months later, I was still unemployed and we were broke. Every job I sought seemed cursed; something would happen that prevented me from getting it. The day I applied for an engineering job at Delco Remy, Delco put a freeze on all hiring.

I applied at a defense contractor in Fort Wayne, one which expressed keen interest. Once again, false hopes; when they learned they were losing their government contract, they too froze hiring.

Despite these disappointments, I considered what occurred at RCA in Marion the cruelest turn of events. They offered me an engineering position but called the next day with an apology, explaining that Thomson Consumer had just purchased RCA and blocked new hires.

The only door not bizarrely shut was the one I didn't want to walk through at the nursing home. I reached a place where I didn't even want to apply for jobs because of the rejection. In retrospect, I see I had mistaken the bizarre for the providential. Sometimes we focus so intensely on our own path that we forget God's; even in our prayers, we can forget to glance at his provisions.

The very job I fought so hard against became one of my greatest blessings. Through my employment with Nationwide Management, I had the opportunity to partner with Larry Maxwell and start our own company, TLC Management. Today TLC has grown to nearly two thousand employees.

I had been upset with God for not providing the preferred job. But those other companies are now closed or have moved. Had I landed one of those jobs, I would have been accepting a lot less than what God had planned for me. I'm now thankful for closed doors, knowing that God's timing is perfect.

It took nine months of unemployment, frustration, loss of self-esteem, financial disaster, a failing marriage, and depression before I surrendered my will to God. While circling the courthouse, I prayed, "God, please give me a job. I will do anything. I will even work in a nursing home." As soon as I prayed that, a peace came over me. I didn't have the job yet, but that day my burden was lifted.

I should have been more faithful, having been raised in a fourth-generation Christian family. My family's faith didn't become mine until attending Expo '72, a Billy Graham Crusade in Dallas, Texas. At that crusade, which occurred during my years at Marion College, I made a decision to follow God and live for him. The journey from the crusade to the courthouse had extreme highs and lows, and though I hope to never experience the latter again in our financial lives, I realize that economic cycles and sudden health-care policies can wreak havoc. But, as trite as it sounds, God is faithful.

The second pivotal event in my life came in the very area that I had made money—health care. This time my own health was in peril. Connie and I had weathered the days of near bankruptcy and various related challenges, but this life-changing event came when the checkbook was fat. Our company had set record profits. A ministry we were heavily engaged in had just closed an extremely positive year. And our daughter had just married a wonderful Christian man. I decided to take our family skiing to celebrate the finish of a great year.

During a tumble on the slopes, I landed on the end of my ski pole. Thinking I had a cracked rib, I went to the emergency room in Vail, where the doctors determined I needed emergency surgery to relieve excessive fluids in my abdominal area. The ski pole, however, was the least of my troubles; they discovered a cancerous tumor in my appendix. In a free fall, I plummeted from the top of the world and slopes celebrating a great year, into the reality of my mortality. This time when I circled the courthouse, so to speak, I was much closer to God, but the conversation was similar—I needed him.

After informing me he couldn't get all of the tumor, the surgeon referred me to an oncology specialist, Dr. Lee (who happened to serve on the Indiana Wesleyan University board). Who not only confirmed the rarity of the cancer, but also recommended Dr. Sugarbaker, a surgeon who had invented a radical surgery for my type of cancer. The next three months brought an extreme test of my faith, as I had to wait to get on Dr. Sugarbaker's docket.

I suppose my fear of the cancer spreading, combined with my years as a CEO, prompted me to keep pressuring him to schedule the surgery sooner. He told me that the best candidate for the grueling surgery was an Olympic athlete. Simply put, I needed the three months to build my strength. I started training every day as if I were running in a marathon—literally as if my life depended on it.

We finally met Dr. Sugarbaker at Washington Hospital Center in D.C. an uninviting urban hospital. He said that if I chose to avoid treatment, I had a zero chance of survival. If I underwent chemotherapy, I would have a 25 percent chance. And if I had his surgery along with heated chemotherapy, the survival rate rose to 66 percent. When I left that day discouraged, I told Connie that I was going to die in that nondescript place.

Back home, I waited another two months for the surgery. I prayed not only for healing, but also for peace. God gave me such peace that at one point I thought I might be in denial about even having cancer.

Even though Connie researched on the Internet and wanted to explain this invasive surgery, I really didn't want to know the details. So when I reported to the hospital the day before the surgery, I was not emotionally prepared for being physically prepped for a colostomy bag. They put a mark on my side where the drain would come out and showed me how to clean and empty the bag. When I expressed shock about having to wear a colostomy bag, they told me they wouldn't know until after surgery if I'd need it. They were preparing me just in case.

The surgery lasted fourteen hours. All my abdominal internal organs were taken out, allowing the surgeon to remove the outer membrane from each organ. With the exception of three that aren't necessary, the organs were put back in place, minus twelve inches of my colon that had to be extracted. Dr. Sugarbaker never took a break during the fourteen-hour surgery. I believe God had his hand on him, because I later learned that he suffered a heart attack during a similar surgery two weeks after mine.

When I awoke, I was in tremendous pain, on a ventilator, and had tubes coming from everywhere, though when I felt for the colostomy bag, it wasn't there. With a surge of adrenaline, I praised God, confident that

I was going to make it. Again, God's timing is perfect. He knew I needed encouragement.

Heated chemotherapy came next. After chemo was pumped into my abdominal area, I had to roll from side-to-side for hours, as if I was activating a washing machine, cleansing my organs.

The first day of the heated chemo treatment was painful. The second day, I felt as if someone had pulled the plug on my energy. The third day, I suffered even more. My insides burned from the membrane removal and the chemo. My mouth bled from sores breaking out on my palate. I signed a living will and told my wife that this is no way to live. *Just let me die.*

The Bible says that in the end times people will cry out to God to let them die (see Rev. 9:6). I believed I was there. As I struggled to collect my thoughts, even to pray for myself, God was saying, "Gary, you don't have to pray. You're all prayed up. And now you have many people praying for you."

During those dark hours, Connie knew I needed encouragement. She arranged for Pastor Steve DeNeff (from College Wesleyan Church in Marion) and Rev. Melvin Maxwell (retired, John Maxwell's father) to pray for me as she held the phone to my ear. Many others stood in the gap, praying for me. I am indebted to all of them, and now, when people ask me to pray for them, I take the request more seriously.

After receiving hundreds of calls, we decided to use a CaringBridge web blog, which kept me connected to the body of believers. I was so encouraged when Connie read the posts from friends and family. Through the blog, we learned that members of a persecuted church I had visited in Belarus were praying and even fasting for me. There aren't more powerful prayers than from those who are being persecuted for Christ.

One of the promises I made to Jesus was that I would use this experience to glorify him. I sometimes wonder why my life was spared and others' lives have been taken. At a more recent men's retreat, I sensed God saying,

"Gary, I gave you six bonus years. What have you done for me?" I tried to think of what he wanted me to do. What can I do now after cancer that I could not do before?

It hit me as if he audibly spoke to me: "It's your grandkids." All of my grandchildren were born after I had cancer. If I had died, I would not have known any of them. I am blessed to have received these bonus years to influence my grandchildren. I am committed to spending quality time with them, teaching them about Jesus and modeling Christian values. They are my legacy and will carry the torch beyond me. But the story was much more than my own desires and joys.

For seven years, I went to my oncologist for checkups. At first it was every three months, then six months, and then annually. I am not a patient person, so spending three hours in the waiting room each visit was challenging. But I learned to turn the waiting into opportunities to minister. Many who shared the waiting room with me weren't going to hear positive news. I hope I was a blessing to them, as they have been to me.

I am now celebrating my ninth "cancerversary." My chances of a recurrence are now the same as anyone who has never had cancer. I would never want to go through it again, but I'm thankful for it, because it changed me. Praise God.

My God is a just-in-time God. He is never early and never late in answering my prayers. He's just in time!

What are your pivotal points? What did you learn? Have you written them for your own reflection, or for your grandkids if you have them? At the least, it's my sincere hope that you're able to use your own pivotal points to help others through theirs.

A LOCAL BOY LOSES IMMUNITIES

WILBUR WILLIAMS

Editor's Note: *One of my favorite college classes was Old Testament with professor Wilbur Williams. This class was also among the toughest—three one-hundred-question tests, and he posted our scores by name in the hall outside his office. That was 1975, and he still teaches that class at Indiana Wesleyan University. He remains a student favorite, voted "professor of the year" nine times. Wilbur was also the first professor I ever met. I had rarely been around a college, let alone face-to-face with a famous professor. My first words to Dr. Williams were, "That's a great picture," pointing to a large antiqued portrait behind his desk. "Is that your great-grandmother?" He looked up from his large worn wooden desk, and, in an echoing voice borrowed from God, replied, "That, young man, is John Wesley." Not the best way to begin at a Wesleyan college. We were meeting in the basement of McConn, the original College Wesleyan Church, converted to offices and a classroom for the Religion Department.*

During the next few years, he became instrumental in my traveling to Israel for a semester to study archaeology, which was formative in my lifelong pursuits. Hundreds of students of the 15,500 he's taught can make similar claims. And he's also taken around 150 tour groups to Israel. Besides owning dozens of rental homes, building a gorgeous replica of a twelfth-century prayer chapel in the center of the campus, and regular jaunts to Jerusalem, he's helped count-less students fall in love with the Old Testament. And he continues his lifelong romance with his wife, Ardelia. I recently ran into Wilbur near campus, while he was driving a truck filled with brush. He had been working with some students he'd hired to help to clear one of his properties. Did I hear him say he'd been up on the roof as well? I'm not certain of his age (I'm not sure he is either), but I'm convinced he's only focused on an eternal calendar.

Although I've spent some sixty years living near Indiana Wesleyan University (IWU), the decade I dedicated to studies in England and New York affected me in more ways than I had anticipated. I was a Grant County boy, born in Gas City, who later moved to Fairmount, and then attended Marion College (now IWU). After graduation, I went to England for graduate studies and then to New York for final studies. It was a joy to return to Marion to begin my teaching career, and here I've stayed.

But my return came with a bizarre downturn in my health. The extended years outside of Grant County had created immunity issues; that is, I lost nearly all immunities! Certain wind-borne dynamics of our local plants wreaked havoc with my system. My nasal passages became perpetually blocked. Breathing was extremely difficult. In addition, I broke out in a serious rash spreading from below my nose to the bottom of my chin. Doctors credited this embarrassing and threatening situation to food allergies; I had grown allergic to peaches, pecans, and crabmeat. I already knew I was allergic to crab—I didn't like it! Various ragweeds and even house dust were also on the allergy list.

My physician finally sent me to the hospital for the dreaded scratch test—a hundred or more small slits in the skin on my back. These tests could identify food and weed allergies. If I was hypersensitive, the cuts

141

would swell. Many of you reading this have been through similar routines or have subjected your children to them. The results determined which blend of fluids they would inject twice weekly. At first they injected a very weak solution. Then through a twenty-five-stage process, I gradually rebuilt as much of my immunities as possible. The doctor informed me that I would possibly continue such a regimen for the remainder of my life.

Many months passed. Nearing the end, when the serum was approaching the final strength, the physician told me to let him know of any unusual reaction. A week or so later, while driving home from the doctor's, I noticed hives blotching my body. Dutifully, I informed my doctor, who provided a treatment. After leaving his office once again, I not only had more severe hives, but I bit my tongue and noticed it was completely numb.

At home I drew a full tub of hot water, hoping to rid myself of the hives. But this sent the serum raging through my body, and I sensed that my head was swelling. My wife called the doctor, who told her, "Get him here as quickly as you can!" It was the longest three miles I have ever taken! Rushed into the doctor's office, I noticed hypodermic needles loaded on both sides of the chair, ready for immediate injection into my arms. My doctor's demeanor had changed—a hidden fright lurked behind his greeting. He chose to remain in his office long after closing hour to ensure the swelling had abated.

After recovering from the episode, I returned to the doctor in much better spirits. In jest I blurted, "I fooled you, didn't I?" He turned to me with the absence of levity. "Wilbur, you were within a half inch of your death! I feared you would arrive unable to breathe, and I had tools ready to perform a tracheotomy. But for some reason, the massive swelling stopped abruptly a half inch from your vocal cords, enabling you to breathe."

On my way home from the doctor's office, I pulled my car to the curb, shut off the motor, then said to God, "I think you may be trying to say something to me. If you are, I am listening." He clearly said to me, "Wilbur, sometimes you act like I don't exist!" I responded, "Lord, I will never look at life the same way again!"

From that time to the present, I have honored that pledge I made to him. It birthed an entirely different man for the next forty-eight years. Being faced with our mortality brings into focus eternal causes, and that's been the center of my career and personal life. Perhaps the metaphor is a stretch, but I think we're all allergic to sin, and it certainly will wreak havoc with our lives.

God gives us enough doses of his glory to see the long view. I've lived in Grant County nearly all my life, but especially since that allergy episode, I've kept in perspective that in God's eyes, I'm only passing through.

MR. HOLLAND'S OPUS
WITH PAINT AND A PONYTAIL

LLOYD E. WOODARD

Editor's Note: Whenever I see Chuck Taylor Converse tennis shoes, especially red ones, I think of Lloyd. From his college days until his early sixties, he has had a Woodstock image, crowned with a receding hairline and long ponytail. We all find him refreshing for the very fact that he is transparent—nothing opaque about Lloyd. From the earring, to the bright shoes with a suit, he is one of a kind. We might say he never left the 1960s, but, truth is, he has never left himself.

The beauty of our church is that whether a top lawyer or hardworking custodian is at the table with Lloyd, all are welcome. He is as predictable as he is steady—basically holding the same job the last couple of decades. He is a highly respected high school art teacher. His superintendent once shared with me that Lloyd had so much more to offer the students than other candidates, from his art skills to being tech savvy, that his hire was an easy choice—one that has served the community well for years. And one last thing about him: he is comfortable in his own skin as a teacher. A few of his artist friends became nationally and internationally acclaimed. One with his fishing and wildlife masterpieces, another with his New York Times bestsellers, and a third with his career illustrating Garfield strips and now Hi and Lois. It's easy to feel lost in one's profession when ensconced by such success, but from my perspective, he celebrates them and they him. In some ways his story may seem common, but that's the beauty of Lloyd, a very uncommon friend.

▼ ▼ ▼

People who know me would probably chuckle if they knew I headed to college with thoughts of being a preacher. I'm not sure my conservative denomination was ready for a hippie, but it seemed the noble path and the right thing to do.

One problem—my heart and mind kept leading me to the artist's palette. I assume that not having a call to the preaching ministry was another sure sign I needed to change majors. It was settled. I really wanted to be an artist—the more well-known, the better. My plan was rather straightforward: graduate from Marion College, move back home to Chicago, and become wealthy and famous.

God's plan, however, was to make me rich in a different way.

Studio artists were cool and they represented the career path for me. So many of my artistic friends seemed to settle for the classroom. Not this independent Chicagoan boy. I had never wanted to be a teacher; I was going to be a studio artist. But when you arrive in a small college in a rural small city, some options simply aren't on the table. It was 1972, and Marion offered only one major in my field—art education. My choices seemed simple: either switch over to the ministry classes (which I knew were not for me), try the teaching classes, or go home.

I stuck with the art major, even though it required several education classes that I would "never need." By the time my senior year rolled around, I was trained and experienced at creating art in a variety of media, and people were buying some of my work. My plans were on track to finish my degree and head back to my hometown. One of the last assignments as an art education major was to apply for teaching positions.

For some reason, I apparently made a good impression—maybe because I had nothing riding on the applications. After all, I wasn't going to be a teacher, so the outcome didn't matter. The first clear indication that God's plans might be different from mine came when I was the first education major in my graduating class to be offered a teaching position. I had college loans to pay and I needed a car and a place to live, so I decided to teach "just for a while." Call it utilitarian theology. Common sense philosophy. Maybe survival. But, I call it providence. God's provision and guidance.

God's plans became a part of me, or I likely would have missed them and him. Soon it seemed like all my job possibilities were in education and studios were no longer an option. After teaching a few years, I devoted an entire summer to pursuing art and design positions in Chicago. Some doors never cracked, and others seemed to shut in my face. Then God orchestrated an amazing vocational teaching moment. A prospective employer whom I had just met summarized the interview with this defining statement: "Lloyd, you're a good artist, but you're an even better teacher."

At summer's end, I returned to Indiana and guess what awaited me? Yep—a teaching job! Only now, instead of a five-minute trip to work, I faced an hour commute. I hated it. I didn't like driving so far in all kinds of weather. I missed time with my family. I never had time for anything else. But God knew it was the only way he could get me to sit still and spend the time with him that I needed to. So every day for months, God and I argued during my commute. Actually, I argued. God just kept on patiently listening, loving me, and using me in spite of myself. I was seeing my job as teaching kids to mix paint and shape clay in exchange for a paycheck. God was speaking through me and reaching out through me to accomplish the work he had for me—making a difference in kids' lives.

Finally, the day came when I got it. God's plans for me included a classroom. I changed from a "me" to a "thee" focus. I sought ways to be more actively involved in God's mission—my teaching position. I started bringing kids to JCBodyshop (student ministries)—hauling them an hour each way on school nights. I made a point of speaking encouragement and hope to the hurting kids around me. When opportunities presented themselves, I was not afraid to share my moral and spiritual positions with students. It's amazing to experience the joy of working with God instead of arguing with him. He began showing me what he was doing in kids' lives and revealing his plan in using me to help restore their hope and ambition for bright futures.

What about my dream of being rich and famous? Perhaps it's the *Mr. Holland's Opus* (Hollywood Pictures) story in real life. From this side of my career, near retirement, I can certainly spot my riches. The riches I often see are being loved and remembered by a throng of students. According to my calculations, I've been blessed to be directly involved in the lives of around thirty thousand students, elementary through college level. My family jokes that anywhere in the world I can bump into a former student. My heart seems to bounce when I'm someplace unfamiliar and I hear a voice calling, "Mr. Woodard!" It's often followed by an enthusiastic hug from a grown-up whom I remember with acne and braces. I hope they still remember me since my vintage ponytail is gone, and I find myself at times without my red Chuck Taylors. I suppose students lock in a picture of the Lloyd they had back then, and I'll always be that age to them. I hope the life lessons and principles of faith will remain just as fresh.

Besides spending time with my own kids, I can't think of a greater joy than reminiscing with "my kids" and hearing about their personal and family milestones and career accomplishments. It especially warms my heart when former students thank me for facilitating their decision to follow Christ.

The whole journey is one of humility and knowing that, even when I wasn't at my best, God could use me. And perhaps I'll hear many yet untold stories in years ahead, or my children will hear them. One such reminder came in a note from a young lady, written a few years after she had passed through my classroom. Her letter began, "Dear Mr. Woodard, thank you for saving my life." She went on to say that in her teens, when she'd had me as her teacher, she had been suicidal. Thanks to God, the love and acceptance she found in my class had given her a reason to hope.

With tears, I thanked God for not giving up on me and for not letting me give up on teaching. I thanked God for continuing to work through me and for offering his love and acceptance to the kids he'd placed in my care, even in the early days when I thought I hated my job.

Accolades and kudos are wonderful. But as I matured, I came to understand that we don't need to know exactly how many lives we've touched or exactly what difference we've made. All we really need to know is that we're where God has placed us and we're doing what God has called us to do. That's not utilitarian theology; it's obedience. We simply trust and obey.

The last season of work came with a much shorter commute, and God allowed me special joy in more involvement in nearby communities. I'll not retire my efforts to help these students, some now in their forties. And though I now have the time and money for that studio artist gig, why settle for just one blessing when you can enjoy the best of both?

PART 6

THE TRUTH OF GOD'S PROVISION

WHEN GOD MOVES MOUNTAINS

MARY CRAMER

Editor's Note: The Bible is replete with God's interaction with people. Sometimes the answer to a prayer is immediate and positive, and other times it's simply not what was hoped for. Maybe it's difficult to ascertain an answer's meaning or understand its delay. Perhaps no topic is as important as fertility or the health and well-being of children. Mary ultimately shares the joyful side of the coin, while giving a glimpse of the other during a season of doubt. This is not an easy subject from any vantage point. Mary's reflections also afford us a glimpse of spiritual routines, a peek into the private side of her habits. While she's thinking through God's words relevant to her journey, she inadvertently prompts us to think about our own journeys and how they intersect with the Bible she values so dearly.

▼ ▼ ▼

During my morning routine, I didn't realize that God was about to reveal something big. It was Tuesday, January 31, 2012, and I was reading the familiar story in Matthew 21: Jesus' withering a fig tree and then telling his disciples that God works through faith-full prayers to move mountains (see vv. 18–22). But this time I was captivated, as if the Holy Spirit was grabbing my attention. My world suddenly revolved around this interaction with God through his Word. I prayed for understanding of what was happening.

My prayer (and train of thought) went something like this: "Wow, to me that seems like a lot of attention to give to that fig tree. The fig tree couldn't be that important in the grand scheme of things, but Jesus used it to make a point. My loving Father, I know that you think of me as more important than the fig tree, and here you tell us that through faith in you mountains can be moved! I believe in your power, and I believe that if it is your will, you will move our mountain. You know our desire to have another child, and we believe it's a desire from you. I am putting my belief and trust in your Word and power."

I sensed God giving me that promise from his Word, and I treasured it in my heart. A little bit later, while in the kitchen, I started to hum a song. I stopped and thought, "Wait, what am I singing?" The lyrics of the chorus from "Mighty to Save" (by Reuben Morgan and Ben Fielding) were running through my mind: "My Savior, he can move the mountains. My God is mighty to save."[1]

My heart swelled with joy; God was again reminding me of his morning promise.

That song and reminder followed me throughout the coming weeks. As I tried to understand this promise on my own, I concluded that God would instantly fulfill this promise; when the next opportunity came around, we would rejoice at seeing a positive pregnancy test. But God had a different lesson in mind.

Anyone trying to conceive knows how harrowing a long wait can be. We had already been trying for seven months. There was nothing fun about this roller-coaster ride, raising our hopes only to see them dashed. One month we had received a positive result only to miscarry a few days later (our second miscarriage overall, but the first within this span). Still

I hoped for those two lines to appear on a pregnancy test and waited eagerly, claiming God's promise. But the weeks came and went, with nothing to celebrate.

Discouragement finally set in along with confusion. Did I misinterpret God's promise? What was he doing? Had I been wrong this whole time? In my searching, God provided answers in unforgettable ways.

Then on Sunday, February 19, full of frustration and hurt due to the negative pregnancy test results, I came to College Wesleyan Church, participating in the service by sitting in the satellite Great Room. I don't think praise and thanksgiving filled my heart as it should have, but that didn't stop God from bulldozing through my self-pity in a mighty way. Pastor DeNeff's message almost caused me to fall out of my chair!

I looked around the room and wondered if others noticed my transparency. It was one of those "just-for-me" sermons. My heart pounded as I soaked in every word about the promises of God. Those words remain as vivid today as they did then.

At the end of the service, Pastor DeNeff asked people to share promises God had given them from his Word. Public speaking or gaining attention is far from my comfort zone. Even the smaller worship venues held more than a hundred people. But then it sank in: this wasn't about me. It was about giving glory to the One who had clearly given me this promise in the first place. He had spoken to me so directly that I was compelled to share. Overcome with this and an overwhelming feeling (that I attributed to the Holy Spirit), I stood and read these words out loud: "But also you can say to this mountain, 'Go, throw yourself into the sea,' and it will be done. If you believe, you will receive whatever you ask for in prayer" (Matt. 21:21–22).

God stunned me that morning, and I'm sure my husband and others, but my soul was encouraged. He had gotten my attention and blasted away my doubt. It was an amazing encounter, and putting my renewed faith into action moved my spirit. I wrote down God's promise. My eighteen-month-old son and I colored a visual reminder: a mountain sinking into the sea. Afterward, we literally stood on the written promise, claiming it for our family. We took that promise and hung it in a prominent place, as a reminder.

A little while later, I listened again to Pastor DeNeff's message on a podcast. I wrote down two main thoughts that encouraged my heart:

1. God gives his promises in the quiet and routine times with him—times when we are in fellowship with him—and he makes something very clear to us in that moment through his Spirit and his Word. Usually we are not even looking for a promise, but his Spirit speaks to our hearts.

2. At times it seems as if everything around us says this promise can't or won't happen. The world says it's impossible. In those times, we need to look to our foundation—Christ. We know that he is our solid rock and his promises cannot fail! If God is for us, who can possibly be against us? When it seems time to give up hope, God calls us to look to him, our rock that is never moved, never shaken—and know he *never* breaks his promises to us!

And God fulfilled his promise. About three months after I read Jesus' amazing words and hid them in my heart, we were rejoicing over a positive pregnancy test. Our second child, a precious daughter, was on her way. We would get to meet her almost one full year after reading God's promise, on an otherwise routine Tuesday morning. God taught me not only about the promises he gives and keeps, but also about his timing and his perfect way, which may be different from my own plans. Yet it is always exactly what I need, exactly when I need it.

God could have stopped there, but he didn't. He knows my heart and his love for me will never cease to amaze me. Along with the positive pregnancy test, he offered another chorus of encouragement that I would be singing over the next eight months: "But when I call on Jesus / All things are possible."[2]

Now every time I hear these songs, they serve as altars of remembrance of what God has done, what he is doing, and what he will do when my faith and hope are in him alone.

NOTES

1. Reuben Morgan and Ben Fielding, "Mighty to Save", MetroLyrics, http://www.metrolyrics.com/mighty-to-save-lyrics-hillsong.html.

2. Nicole C. Mullen, "Call on Jesus," MetroLyrics, http://www.metrolyrics.com/call-on-jesus-lyrics-nicole-c-mullen.html.

WAITING FOR GRACE
A JOURNEY THROUGH BARRENNESS

ANDREW SPROCK

Editor's Note: *When our wait for divine answers stretches beyond the foreseeable future, even longer than a decade, we can chronicle many lessons. We can identify with great moments of joy, unknown depths of frustration, new definitions of patience, and a litany of awkward scenarios. In the Sprocks' story below, imagine if this book had gone to print in year ten of their journey to the conception of their daughter, instead of in year eleven. Where would God have been in that story? Perhaps you'll find below about as clear of an answer as one could glean from sharing such a journey. Depending on the size of your church or how long you've worshiped there, people around you each Sunday likely represent the full continuum in this parenting journey. In this book, we find couples that never experience the surprise at year eleven. We find parents surprised to be raising unexpected grandchildren. And parents whose answer to years of prayers are children with special needs. As we experience Andrew's remarkable openness, we realize that often the answer comes not when we need it, but when it needs us.*

▼ ▼ ▼

Eleven years ago our hearts were fertile with hope. Having been married three years, we had just finished seminary together and were ready to embrace a new adventure, becoming parents. Expectant of new life, we were unprepared for the long and desolate journey ahead.

I remember the descent into the valley of barrenness. The dip in the path felt subtle, almost imperceptible, after the first month. "Well, we must have been off on the timing. That's OK. We have time." Two, three, six, eleven months passed. The path we were walking now had a noticeable decline.

Silly things, like the agreement we had made with a good friend that we would have a baby as soon as he got married, lost their humorous edge. He got married. We weren't having a baby.

Questions began to overshadow our dismissive "There's always next month." The questions in the earlier months had been hard but still marked by hope: What do we need to do differently? Are there some dietary changes or vitamins that might help? Timing? Temperature?

Twelve months had passed. There was officially a term for people who had come this far: *infertile*. In some ways, the label brought relief. It somehow legitimized our struggle. It felt a bit like an unbiased spectator saying that our path was really hard. We were having difficulty articulating just how devastating it was to deal with eroding hope. The word *infertile* gave us language to talk about our pain. We wanted to hold a new life; instead, we held hope and a helpful rubric. We resented the jokes of others: "I barely did much more than look at my wife and we got pregnant." The path grew darker.

With the official diagnosis of infertility we could start seeking medical intervention and we did. After a battery of tests, the medical experts concluded that there were some challenges, but none that should prevent us from conceiving. Over the course of the next months, we reluctantly yet desperately submitted ourselves to the unnatural and invasive. Maybe

God was doing this to increase our trust and reinforce how miraculous the creation of life is. How much more of this was necessary before God was convinced that we were appropriately grateful? We confessed that our faith could use some refining, but this was beginning to feel more antagonistic than loving.

It seemed that we were too often the ones chosen when people wanted to confide the trauma of an accidental pregnancy. We didn't have much sincere empathy to offer. The path became not only darker, but bleak. We were lost. We stopped going to baby showers or celebrating babies at all. Rather, we nursed the sting felt when yet another friend or family member announced a pregnancy. Resentment and despair crowded out any visible markings of the trail of hope. Prayer in that season was silent—except for when we were laying bare our mistrust or accusing God of being harsh. We were lost, and a storm had settled in!

As we groped for anything that could hold us steady, we realized that hope, faith, trust, and the knowledge that we were loved, had at some point been lost or severely compromised. We tried to recount those graces that had at one time anchored us, even though their reality seemed distant.

Our relationship also felt the pressure. As much as we tried to comfort and encourage each other, at times our sorrow and disappointment were aimed at each other. After one such encounter, I left the house to go for a walk. I was so angry and hurt. As I stormed through the neighborhood, my message to God was terse: "If this is what it means to be loved by you, I don't want any part of it!"

I found myself in the neighborhood of a Catholic church and school where I had taught a few years earlier. I stopped, intending to ask the priest, a man I respect and trust, to defend God. The familiar office staff warmly greeted me as I entered, and they surprised me with their genuine interest in my well-being. I felt cared for and missed by them in a way I hadn't expected. The exchange softened me a bit and I eventually asked if

Father Bob was available. Of course he was out! That was completely consistent with our experience of God in this valley. God seemed nowhere in sight when we were most desperate and alone. The storm that had calmed a bit as I visited with the office staff churned up. I closed the conversation as politely as I could manage and left. I nearly ran into a man as I burst out the door. There was Father Bob!

I turned back around and stormed along beside him. As we sat down in his office, I jumped right in. I came on strong and forced myself to rein in my impatience. Father Bob wasn't the accused; God was. But then I dismissed the hesitation and blasted ahead. Coming to a stopping point, I gave Father Bob a chance to offer a rebuttal. He didn't. I had made some harsh accusations against the God he was supposed to represent. He made no defense and actually seemed moved. He sat in the chair; the diatribe had clearly burdened him. Feeling our sorrow, he offered no explanation. This was not what I was looking for! I couldn't help but feel softened by his response, but there was enough venom in me to mount one more strike. I tried again, hoping I could rile him to defend God so I could crush his argument with the insurmountable pile of evidence.

Father Bob continued to listen. Instead of refuting my evidence and affording me the opportunity to crush his response, he had moved over to stand with me. He offered few words, only ones that let me know he was hurting with us. If he was going to stand with us under this mound of evidence against God, I wanted him to be angrier. At the least he could help me throw rocks heavenward. But he did not. We hugged and then I walked past the office staff on my way out. They again affirmed how good it was to see me, how I was missed at the school. They didn't know why I was there, but they extended their well wishes for Melissa and me.

As I walked across the church parking lot toward home, I began to weep uncontrollably. I had not been given the answer I wanted, but I had been given the thing my heart needed most. God heard us! God was weeping with us! I wanted some promise that the thing we had exhausted ourselves hoping for was going to come to pass. We were given no such promise, but God was with us. God had heard us. We were not alone!

The darkness began to lift, even while we were still trudging through the valley.

In the weeks and months after that, we found the questions and sorrow to be no less present. It was still so wearing to wander this path, but anger and loneliness no longer devoured us. It seems that the piercing eyes of doubt have a harder time attacking a group, because that is who we walked with now. As God's tenderness with us had clarified our need not to be alone on this journey, we began to share more with our family and closest friends. God had given us a fellowship of brothers and sisters who knew our story and walked with us. They let us cry and cried with us. They slowed down when we found ourselves weary. By their presence, they encouraged us to hope, but, in truth, they were the ones who carried it for us most often. They carried our sorrow, too. There was far more of that than we could endure alone, so they divided that among them and carried it as well.

We stopped and asked our traveling mates to circle up with us at our home, to pray for us, for healing, for the longing of our hearts. With these friends gathered around us, it was a child who first broke the silence. We were led in prayer by a nine-year-old. Not only were our friends carrying this with us; so were their families. The children whom God had given them became blessings to us. These children hoped with us. Something about a child praying for our childbearing stirred us deeply. The boy was bold, compassionate, hopeful, and without hesitation—on our behalf.

The journey we shared with these friends eventually buoyed us enough that we entered into the adoption process. Six years after we had started trying to have a child, we got the call that a birth mother had chosen us. A few weeks later, we became parents. It was not in the way we expected, but our hearts could not have been fuller. Once again, it was more than we could bear on our own, and our traveling companions passed around our joy, multiplying it and celebrating with us. We named our son Malakai, "Messenger of God." God's message to us was now tangible in the son in our arms.

It was confusing to be so full of gratitude and yet still bear the weight of our grief and longing to conceive. Eventually, what seemed like a contradiction became our reality. We, together with our traveling mates, carried joy and sorrow, gratitude and longing, fulfillment and hope unfulfilled.

Three years later, nine years after we started trying to have children, we adopted our second son. His name, Tobias, means "God Remembers." Joy was again multiplied in our midst. We danced, prayed, cheered, and embraced again, overflowing with gratitude.

We were delighted with the family God had given us. We were full. There remained alive in us some of the questions about conception. Whether we had just become accustomed to carrying sorrow or whether it in fact got lighter I can't really say, but it was still with us. We reconciled ourselves to the reality that this particular sorrow, the sorrow of not being able to conceive and bear a child, might always be with us. This was the path we were to walk, and it was familiar. Our legs had been strengthened and we no longer felt the perpetual weariness. This was our journey.

Occasionally, our church service ends with an invitation to renew our hope. This past December, the directness of that message was different. The Advent-season service had centered on the wait of Zechariah and Elizabeth. An angel appeared to Zechariah, affirming that he and Elizabeth need not fear because God had heard their prayer (see Luke 1:13). Their prayer was ours. They, too, were barren. The clarity with which the sermon and the story spoke to our story was undeniable. Pastor DeNeff said:

What is it that you have been waiting a long time for and you still don't have? . . . What is it that you have wanted that has just taken the wind out of your sails? So that you, like Zechariah, came to the place where you said, "You know what? Maybe I misinterpreted that. Maybe this is just the way it is going to be; this is as good as it gets." I'm telling you this morning, this is not as good as it gets. There is a time in our lives where God will say, "I know what you want. I have heard it. I will give you the desires of your heart." In a moment, I'm going to give you a chance to say it again. I want you to say it again, because I think some of us have just quit saying it. We don't ask for it anymore. It just taunts us.[1]

He ended by talking about hope being conceived when we hear God say to us that our prayers had been heard. We reluctantly went forward, daring to hope. What we did not yet know was that more than hope was conceived that week.

Weeks later we found out we were pregnant. We could hardly believe it! It had been eleven years since we had started trying to conceive. Now we had come to a portion of the trail completely unfamiliar. We didn't know how to respond, so we kept quiet.

Toward the end of one appointment late in the first trimester, the nurse asked Melissa if we had told anyone. We had not. She encouraged us to tell. "Whether or not your high-risk pregnancy lasts, you'll need support." Of course we would! Why had we not thought of it like that? We had been journeying that way for so long, so why would we not let our journeying mates join us here, too? So we shared our news.

The joy, tears, and wonder that we saw reflected in friends and family loosened something in us—the doubt and skepticism that this really could be for us.

Oddly, the baby for whom we had waited so long was not easy for us to grasp. And so again, our friends held baby Karis with us. In the birthing room, they passed her around and let loose the joy that was beyond our capacity. On one level, they were less surprised than we were, for they had been carrying a larger portion of hope for us. In every case, their joy and wonder freed us to embrace the reality that our path had changed.

Early on in our infertility, Melissa started writing letters in her journal to a yet-unknown little girl named Karis, which means "grace." It has been years since either of us had really spoken or written to her, feeling so distant from the kind of hope that would allow us such intimate communication. Today, with the retelling of this story, we mark the renewal of that journal.

Dearest Karis,

You are a gift more overwhelming than you could ever know. We, your parents, your brothers, and the many who have loved us and you along the way are so delighted with your arrival. May you know most intimately the God who hears us and who is with us. Our dear daughter, our grace, you are here! At long last, you are here!

NOTE

1. Steve DeNeff, "Fear Not: In the Wait of Our Despair" (sermon, College Wesleyan Church, Marion, IN, 12/07/2014).

PRAYER ON THE TITHE ENVELOPE

KEITH AND SHARON DRURY

Editor's Note: *One of the mysteries of life is the fate of children, and it's hard to comprehend God's decisions with the lives of the innocent. This side of heaven, we'll not fully understand why some are spared and some go to heaven at an early age. It was with rather mixed emotions that I prepared this chapter. On the one hand, anything from the Drurys is an honor to handle. They have influenced many thousands of pastors through their journeys. Sharon exudes a class and a steadiness that balances her husband's eccentricities and maverick forays. She also helped shape a key part of Indiana Wesleyan University. It's hard for me to think of Keith's influence and not recall one spontaneous moment in the dingy basement of McConn Church. He listened to a student's convoluted question about his various ministry opportunities, then turned and drew a V on the chalkboard. He proceeded to articulate the notion that your life is like a wedge, the narrower and sharper, the deeper impact you'll make. Twenty years later, with his permission and attribution, that genius notion became the fulcrum of my books with McGraw-Hill. His "strategetics" are also brilliant and help capture important concepts with simple images. His* Tuesday Column *blog has drawn thousands of readers. Many know him for* Holiness for Ordinary People, *the bestselling book published by Wesleyan Publishing House.*

Nevertheless, as excited as I was to receive an entry from the Drurys, their topic nags at my attempt at peace. While writing this, doctors informed our oldest son, Jason, that his first child will live only a short while. He and his wife, Hope, had such joy and excitement until that fateful ultrasound. We concur with their refusal for abortion and are pleased they are carrying the baby until delivery.

For those of you reading the exciting story below about a child's survival but have experienced different outcomes like our family's, the joy is that God allows any of us to have the blessing of children and grandchildren. Especially in the body of Christ, we rejoice when children not only survive, but also thrive. The son mentioned below is now a philosophy professor and Princeton trained, like his father. And he's helped to bring a wave of young Princetonians to teach at Indiana Wesleyan University, including his wife, the prolific author Amanda Drury.

There is much that eludes me as I read this story, and I take 1 Corinthians 13:12 at face value, "We see through a glass, darkly" (KJV). But, as Dr. Glenn Martin, a mutual friend of mine and the Drurys, would often say, "Remember this, my friend, we do see through the glass. We see enough to know the truth." And walking in the truth, we trust God with our children (see 3 John 4).

▼   ▼   ▼

It was a normal Tuesday morning until our ten-year-old son, John, showed up at the breakfast table with his eye bulging out from its socket like a Halloween mask. He wasn't crying but was mystified. I called the pediatrician, who insisted that we bring him in right away. When we showed up in her office, she bypassed the examination and urgently instructed, "Take him immediately to the hospital and I'll meet you there."

She warned that infection in the eye could easily migrate to the brain. Now amply worried, we signed him into the ER, where she linked us to an

ENT surgeon. He rushed in to perform the emergency surgery to remove an infected sinus-cavity cyst. We slept better that night, but by morning the eye had swollen even worse.

When the surgeon arrived the next morning, he shook his head. "The surgery simply didn't get it all, and the brain scan shows it's still there. He needs to go to Riley Children's Hospital in Indianapolis immediately." Transferring to that busy children's hospital meant that John couldn't get into surgery until after midnight.

Our hearts ached as we watched our weakened son being wheeled into surgery; we would have gladly taken his place on that gurney if possible! But this surgery didn't work either; the brain scan showed the mass of infection growing. We struggled to keep our fear in check.

When our church mentioned this prayer concern on Sunday morning, a man we didn't know had heard the request and felt God say, "Go pray for that boy." Bob Hendricks wasn't a fancy man, but he knew it was God speaking. He felt compelled to write a little prayer on a tithe envelope and drive a hour and a half to the Indianapolis hospital. Finding us standing in the room with our friends, Bob simply announced, "God told me to come down and read this prayer for John."

We gathered in a circle around John's bed. Bob read his rough but simple prayer off the tithe envelope, said good-bye, and left. The next day, as the surgeon was scheduling a third surgery, he stopped by, examined John, cocked his head, and said, "We'd better do another CT scan."

Within an hour, he returned to the room shaking his head, saying, "Well, the mass has completely disappeared . . . well, sometimes these things happen."

Yes, they do, and praise God!

MIRACULOUS INTERVENTION

DAVID KELLY

Editor's Note: We sometimes attend church with wonderful, positive people, not knowing that they have been to the gates of hell and back. I know the young Kellys through their steady parents, and we often all share the same pew. I've just assumed they spent their lives on the Yellow Brick Road. It's a reminder of the power of the gospel, of its message that transcends young and old families and a wide range of economic, health, and emotional conditions. It speaks into our humanness with a hope in something that is otherworldly. David's story has that unforgettable moment of prayer with a person of God that invokes miracles. We all long for access to such a prayer warrior. We all long for answers of miraculous healing for ourselves or loved ones. We are encouraged when we read stories like David's, accounts that heighten our hope and encourage us to accept the promise of eternal bliss when healing on this side of heaven is someone else's story.

▼   ▼   ▼

The doctor's words cut deep: "There is no cure." It was like waking up in a nightmare. I would be like this for the rest of my life? I was in a psych ward meeting with doctors and therapists all day, every day, trying to unravel the mystery: what had happened to my sanity? Slowly draining from me for ten years, it had finally vanished. I had lost the ability to control my emotions.

The symptoms included bouts with depression, rage against my wife, and suicidal thoughts. Sometimes I would have a turnaround and be the "life of the party," happy and energized, barely needing to eat or sleep for days. But before long, I would sink back into debilitating depression, unable to function or get out of bed. On my worst days, I experienced blackouts and short-term memory loss.

Whatever I thought my life was going to be, I was wrong. The doctor told me that I had been misdiagnosed ten years earlier: when I woke up gasping in my sleep each night, it hadn't been panic attacks, but, rather, sleep apnea. I had been almost suffocating in my sleep each night for nearly a decade, and now my brain had suffered irreparable damage and would no longer correctly produce the chemicals needed to regulate emotions.

They diagnosed me as bipolar, with other undetermined issues, such as memory loss. And so began the many months of hospital stays, medication trials and adjustments, and a marriage that was falling apart, not to mention my two young sons who really didn't have a father anymore. During one hospital admission, doctors gave me more bad news: one of the medications had damaged my kidneys. Now, on top of everything else, with only 50 percent kidney function, I would have to be under the watchful eye of a kidney specialist for the rest of my life.

It was all too much, so I decided to end my life. When my wife, Maria, realized my intentions, she called the doctor, and I found myself locked up in the psych ward. At this same time, Maria's brother Marty was facing a battle of his own: cancer. He was only thirty-seven years old, a nonsmoker, and had rededicated his life to God in a magnetic way. But intense prayer support and personal faith did not turn back the disease, which eventually took his life.

His peaceful outlook gave me hope when I was released from the hospital. Though many continued to pray, my condition deteriorated. Then something unexpected happened during a trip to Florida. A friend introduced me to her pastor, encouraging me to tell this stranger my life story, which I did. When I finished, he said, "I believe that if I pray for you today, you will be healed."

Many people had prayed for my healing. While I thought God *could* heal me, I didn't really think he *would*. At least, not until I was in heaven. Otherwise, he would have done so by then. But, eager for all the prayer I could get, I told him he could pray for me. As the man prayed, God met me and I heard him speak. It wasn't in an audible voice. In my spirit, I heard God say, "If you want to be well, then you'll be well." It was that simple. All I had to do was say it. And so, I said, "I do! I want to be well." And, like that, I was. God had miraculously intervened. He had calmed my troubled waters. He had parted my Red Sea. He had healed me.

In the weeks and months that followed, the doctors were baffled as they confirmed there was no sign of brain damage, no sign of sleep apnea, and no sign of kidney damage. One medical professional told me, "This can only be explained by miraculous intervention." God had given us a new hope for the future.

And so began the process of rebuilding a marriage and learning to live without the mental illness that had plagued me for years. God did restore our marriage and bring healing to our family. So significant was our family's transformation that when people would hear our story years later, they couldn't picture it as described. It simply didn't match the person they saw in front of them.

But one question remained for us: why did God heal me, but let Marty die? I asked God how he could allow suffering when he has the power to stop it, and why he healed some and not others. I asked, "How is Marty's dying good for him on any level?" The answer came, "If you could ask Marty that right now, he could explain it to you."

I understood. God really did know better than I did. Sin entered the world, and thus suffering happens. But God is good and he loves us. He parts seas, calms waters, and parts the heavens so dying saints can see his glory. God loves us even when we can't see it.

DIVINE HELP AND
DIVINELY APPOINTED HELPERS

BUD AND JUDY LEACH

Editor's Note: *Have you ever met a seemingly timeless couple? Besides the graying of their hair, thirty-five years later they seem unchanged. The way they move. The laughter. Their consistent help in the faith community. That's the Leaches. After returning from missionary service in Sierra Leone, they helped me found the JCBodyshop (student ministries) in 1981. Along with them and a few other couples, we started the program with a group of eight kids. Within a few years we were involved in the discipleship and outreach of hundreds. I'm convinced that the deepest longtime friends are those with whom you're involved in sustained ministry. Judy is a nurse and Bud an engineer. Both are brilliant and as consistent as Ronald Reagan's economics. Judy led the very first discipleship group for JCBodyshop. I can still see her driving away from our former church building in 1982 in their old station wagon, loaded with teen girls. It was the first of a large network of such groups. I recall the day I showed up in the Body Shop to find unique café-style booths, which Bud had designed and built with others during the night. Another time he drove through the night from Flint, Michigan, to Marion, Indiana, and back, because I had failed to put the bus registration in the glove box, and we were going across the Canadian border in the morning with a large group of teens. I learned of this sacrifice twenty years later.*

He seems to walk in slow motion, often with sliding trousers on his thin frame, with a shirt winning the constant battle to be untucked on one side. And Judy has that perpetual soft, classy look. That is, no matter what she wears, she wears it well. Politely professional. Their kids are a joy, the fulcrum of their lives—next to Christ and his church. Bud even helped design the strikingly beautiful new College Wesleyan Church, especially its functionality (no unused space—there are storage units in the most creative places).

You likely have a couple in mind in your church that serve like the Leaches. To be a true fit, you'd always picture their faces with inviting smiles. Bud's with somewhat of a southern tilt. Judy's with a full view of youthful teeth. Both are ageless and priceless.

▼ ▼ ▼

Although we've entered our golden years, we're fortunate to still recall with vivid appreciation and joy some golden memories. Two themes have infused our lives together, and we'll touch briefly on them: God's sustaining power through physical healing, and God's empowerment for ministry through relationships. We'll treat each in turn, but they're really inseparable.

We don't know why God heals some and not others, but we know he has healing power. We were living in Sierra Leone. Our son wasn't potty trained, which was a hardship in itself. But when he developed malaria-like symptoms at two-years-old and didn't respond to treatments, we went into crisis mode. He was on the brink of death before a providential accident saved his life.

All the kids and Bud had contracted malaria at some point, so we knew the drill. We started him on malaria treatments. We fortunately lived near the hospital, where the staff ran all the normal labs, but nothing worked. He maintained a high temperature—104 to 105 degrees. With sporadic electricity, keeping him cool proved difficult. When Bud found a generator, we could at least keep fans going.

Would he live or die? We didn't know. After ten sleepless nights, we knelt by his bed exhausted. We had to commit him to the Lord: "God, you gave us this little boy, and if you're taking him back now, that's obviously not what we want, but we'll trust you."

Two days after that prayer, an accident that seemed like "the last straw" actually saved his life. We had received a crate from the States, which remained on our porch. Though our son still had a high fever, his curiosity drew him outside, to explore that crate. In typical toddler style, he carelessly knocked over the crate's lid and suffered a deep cut on his leg from its nails. When the wound became infected, we administered antibiotics.

A remarkable healing followed, and not just for the infection. The fever left and he recovered. Antibiotics were not the prescribed treatment for malaria. Only the Great Physician understood the underlying diagnosis and proper prescription. Almost lost in this miraculous recovery is that he potty trained himself. A bonus for a mother!

Two decades later, God again brought miraculous healing to our family. After living in Marion, Indiana—Bud's hometown—for some years, we moved to Columbus, Ohio, for Bud's job. While there, we received devastating news: Bud needed surgery for a brain tumor. Even though we weren't members of College Wesleyan Church at the time, Bud called Steve DeNeff, the new pastor, whom we had known as a student.

"Can you look after my mother, who's very distressed about 'her little boy'?" Bud asked. Steve not only agreed, but also called Bud the day before his surgery and prayed for him. Our friends from our youth sponsor days— Dennis, Lois, and Joy—came and spent the day at the hospital, caring for us with tangible love. So many people called us. The children's Sunday school classes sent an avalanche of cards. The outpouring of love from College Wesleyan Church members is permanently impressed in our spiritual diaries. We know that church community knows no walls. No state or country boundaries. No limits. The surgery and treatments were successful.

We don't know how God chooses certain people to be in our lives, or what role we play in choosing, but we do know that God uses relationships to sustain us.

One of those special relationships developed around fuel and tanks, of all things. During our first five months in Africa, Bud oversaw the delivery of diesel for the Kamakwie hospital compound. One task loomed large: authorities said that storage tanks had to be buried or put in a concrete building.

Burying the tanks seemed problematic. The Kamakwie ground is full of iron. If you dig up a pile and expose it to rain, it rusts and turns into stone. So Bud worked with his assistant, Sebe, to add a twelve-foot concrete-block extension onto a workshop. For ventilation, he added some louvered blocks in one wall, finishing the project just three days before a big storm—our first African rainy season. We had no idea what we were in for.

We couldn't believe the damage. The wind had blown the roof off the new building, and the reinforced-concrete wall had imploded. Sebe, who became Bud's right-hand man, surveyed the damage and quietly said, "I thought this was going to happen." After prompting, he identified the problem: the airflow holes in the concrete walls. Once the door was locked, they allowed in a breeze, which had nowhere to escape. "So it blew off the roof."

"Why didn't you tell me?" Bud asked.

Sebe explained that they did everything "the master's" way first, and then if that didn't work, they'd try something else.

Bud immediately replied, "I am not your master; Jesus Christ is. And I am here to work alongside you, not above you." Their relationship grew strong. Forty years after our mission term ended in Sierra Leone, we returned, and this side-by-side relationship is still close, like we had never left.

God has shown us grace through healing and helpers. We could list many more occasions of each. We've used John 15:16 as an operational verse throughout our time in Africa, and really, all our lives. "You did not choose me, but I chose you and appointed you so that you might go and bear fruit— fruit that will last—and so that whatever you ask in my name the Father will give you." Wherever we've been, and whatever we've done, God has been there with us. He's enabled us to do his work. He's provided for us and our faith in him has grown with each passing day.

JOURNEY OF THE HEART

CHERYL (LUTTRULL) RYAN

Editor's Note: Perhaps nothing is more traumatic than losing a child. But losing one's heart, figuratively or literally, also ranks among life's toughest passages. The following story from Cheryl Ryan chronicles her amazing journey through all of these losses. Her unique dimension is processing the gift of a new, life-sustaining heart—one that came from a donor about the age of the daughter she lost in a tragic auto accident. Cheryl somehow manages to reflect on lessons learned, maintaining a hopeful expectation for what's ahead.

The backstory here is that she comes from one of the most respected families in the church and community. Her parents have been second parents to many of us at some season, including our college days, when her father served as the dean of Indiana Wesleyan University. Her parents live in the same house they occupied when I met them in the 1970s, a historic beauty downtown. A few blocks away, her brother's family have lived in the same type of home for decades; he serves as a multiple-term county prosecutor. Her sister has been a valued social worker in the area throughout her career. For many in our county, and for most among our longtime church members, her family is inextricably linked to the very mention of College Wesleyan Church.

Imagine the widespread concern and interest in the events Cheryl relates below. I remember the first day I saw her back at work, sharing the same desk as my wife—warmly greeting people as they entered the church office. Cheryl has another feature common among her Luttrull roots—eyes that offer a glimpse into her soul. There was a sparkle in those facial windows, and I couldn't help but return a smile that stretched back decades.

⟩ ⟩ ⟩

It was a typical Thursday at work when my heart stopped. Lunchtime had been busy, and I was showing a potential client the Hostess House, a historic mansion in Marion, about a block from my parents' home. The air conditioning was on the fritz again, and I had been running up and down the three flights of stairs all day. I was exhausted. What's more, the hot, stuffy air exacerbated my asthma.

During one pass between the expansive rooms, I paused to lean against the door frame. Suddenly the world was spinning out of control. Was I trapped in a dream? From above, I seemed to be watching a slow-motion video. People rushed around the person spread on the floor—and that person was me. Usually I was alone in the Hostess House at 3 p.m., but this day there was a doctor, nurse, and even a dentist, and soon ambulance personnel.

I had thought I was invincible. I worked hard, for long hours, but fully enjoyed my managerial position. All of this changed in an instant. In one moment, I was taken from being an active, social, outgoing person, to being flat on my back. I seemed to have one foot in another world and one very much planted here. I insisted that my husband, Kenny, take me to the local hospital a few blocks away. We hoped to avoid ambulance charges. I was not thinking clearly, of course. The ambulance crew was already at hand. Even so, we drove ourselves. I would later come to recognize my severe phobia of ambulances resulting from the earlier loss of my daughter in a car accident.

As the doctors and technicians visited my hospital room, it was still as if someone else was the subject of this drama. After various tests, they shared shattering news: unbeknownst to me, I had previously experienced a silent heart attack that had rendered half of my heart dead. Now the other half was experiencing atrial fibrillation; they were sending me to CCU. My immediate family and many from my extended family had arrived; we don't believe in going through things alone! Although the doctor wanted me to wait several days for the St. Vincent heart catheterization team's routine visit to Marion, my daughter wouldn't accept this plan. She moved mountains to get me moved to Indianapolis.

Two stents and a defibrillator later, I was beginning my "journey of the heart." We are defined by our history and I had gone from being an energetic daughter, wife, and mother, and along the way, a working woman. My attention remained outward. Suddenly, I had to learn to be someone who was totally self-focused and dependent on others. The changes were many and sudden, including the shift from two incomes to one. Between my limitations, huge medical expenses, and numerous visits to doctors an hour away in Indianapolis, it took Kenny and me a long while to get our bearings.

My journey of the heart was eased by the support from College Wesleyan Church, sending cards and letters, calling and visiting. This had been my home church since I was six, but I had moved away in physical and spiritual ways without even noticing. Somehow my heart had lost its way. I believe God laid me flat on my back to make me look again to the heavens. It wasn't an instant awakening, but a gradual return as I was quieted and could once again listen. I read the Bible and insightful books people gave me. Wonderful church women sat, listened, talked, prayed, and cried with me for hours on end. Joan Bardsley (see pp. 200–203), who was going through training for Soul Coaching, adopted me. The timing was perfect. I'm not sure we followed the curriculum, but our sessions led to a godly friendship. I was finally learning to *listen*, which had never been easy growing up—always vying for the last word. I suppose part of this was the way God designed me, but I'm also sure he delighted in quieting me, if only for a while.

The next sixteen months were turbulent. Eventually doctors said I needed a heart transplant or LVAD (heart pump). The team decided that I could not handle the LVAD surgery; I was to stay in the hospital, receiving life-extending medicines until a heart became available—or I lost my battle. This prognosis was quite traumatic for the family, but I felt strangely enveloped with otherworldly peace. I don't know if it was my faith as a whole, or simply the knowledge that if I died I would see my daughter, Holly, in heaven. Whatever the outcome, I was ready. As my energy flagged, the nurses continued to flood me with bag after bag of medicine, and my family stayed by my side constantly.

Early on Friday, January 13, 2012, one of my cardiologists, Dr. Schleeter, walked in and sat right on the bed. He looked so serious; I thought he was going to say they had decided just to let me go home and die. Instead, he shocked me by saying, "I've found you a heart."

"What?" I'd hardly been able to anticipate hearing those words. The donor was a twenty-one-year-old who had suffered a stroke, a malady unrelated to a heart problem, so I was not to worry about the organ's viability. In the ensuing hours, allowing time for the heart to arrive from an undisclosed location, questions consumed me. Was the donor male or female? Did this person have a close family? Having lost a sixteen-year-old daughter fourteen years earlier, I was aching for the parents. Did I have the right to celebrate the continuation of my life at the expense of a young person?

The exhausting details of the surgery prep afforded me limited processing time. Did tests still show that I qualified for this young heart? After an all-clear, my newly implanted heart was started at 11:04 p.m.

on Friday, January 13, 2012. For me, there was nothing unlucky about the day.

The journey has been long and eventful and is still in process. One week after the transplant, my lungs gave out. Every breath felt as if I was drowning. Every time I closed my eyes, I sensed a full-color horror movie. I couldn't describe my distress, and my family could only plead with the nursing staff to help and intervene. As it turned out, among other things, I had a pulmonary embolism. A huge blood clot was trying to wrap itself around my new heart. I remember my two transplant surgeons running to my bed through the hallways of the hospital yelling "hold the 'vator, hold the 'vator!" Another open-chest surgery later, I was back on the road to healing.

At least three near-death episodes and various blackouts opened a window into my soul. Two and a half slow years followed, riddled with healing, inconvenient restrictions, interminable doctor visits and tests, and handfuls of pills to sustain life. I had to avoid contact with people and wear a mask. My steroid-swollen face and neck required adjustments, to say nothing of the multiple other side effects of my medications. I experienced dramatic emotional fluctuations: laughing, yelling, crying, and then cyclical guilt for the outbursts. My wonderful husband, family, and friends all learned to duck and roll with the changes.

Through it all, I've experienced and learned a great deal about unconditional love. Not only from Kenny and my daughter Heather, but also from family and friends, especially the congregation of College Wesleyan Church. I am so thankful for the encouragement that was an integral part of my healing process. I have come a long way and am now working for this wonderful church part time. I'm part of a team helping others, once again a true part of the community. God is working with me daily to fully appreciate my extended life.

My faith shows incremental, but daily, growth. I never again want to be a surface Christian, but be wholly and deeply grounded in the Word, a servant of our Lord and Savior, consistent in making a difference in small ways that matter. My heart continues on this special journey, and I thank God that I have the opportunity to be whatever and wherever he has planned.

PART 7

THE **TRUTH**
OF **GOD'S**
PURPOSE

A DAY THAT WILL LIVE IN ETERNITY

DON A. GLENN

Editor's Note: Conversations with Don always prove soothing. He's probably had a gentleman's posture and demeanor since the crib. In some ways, vocally, he's a pastoral duplicate of Frank Sinatra or Barry White, predictably calming. And when he begins to laugh, his eyes squint and glisten, and simultaneously his cheeks blush and turn the hue of his hair. I picture Don much like Catherine Marshall describes Peter in her noted book A Man Called Peter. *That is, a man with his routines, such as gardening, and one with whom neighbors would chat over the fence whenever they could steal his ear. Marshall also noted he'd be gardening in a dress shirt and perhaps a tie.*

I first met Don thirty-five years ago at a rather rustic church camp in Rockford, Illinois. His hair had a unique auburn wave across his forehead that seemed to be the crown of a saint. I also found his son, Scott, to be a reflection of his father's goodness. Scott is a high-functioning special-needs son. When I saw Scott recently on a holiday, attending church with his father, he once again made me feel as if I was the center of the universe. From our camp days until now, he always called my name, looked me straight in the eyes, and had a deliberate word of encouragement. That's certainly his dad coming through. The same enjoyment comes from Don's daughter, Pam, who holds a PhD but remains perpetually humble and focused on others. Considering she has a rare degree in the nursing field and is a university dean, her servant's heart is all the more magnified. (Can one inherit such qualities?)

The following contribution is "old school." That is, it affords a glimpse into one of the great revival eras of American Christianity. It also peeks at theology, trying to frame one's spiritual journey into sensible categories. But more than any of this, it allows us to saunter through Don's lifelong fascination with his Savior. You come to the end knowing that if you ever needed to talk with a living saint, well, you'd certainly be hard pressed to do better than one from the old school.

▼ ▼ ▼

I have rarely done what I am about to do—tell you my story. This is not in my character because I do not wish to seem larger than life. Neither do I wish to make myself appear to be something I am not. Whatever good is found in this story is of God. So against this backdrop, I offer you a glimpse of my life's story—its thesis. Every January 26, I observe the anniversary of my "new birth," and I have done so since 1950, when my soul was saved and my life completely redirected.

Some decisions have lasting ramifications, but only one has eternal consequences. Whatever my life has become in this temporary world, before God, I can share with you that it all revolves around this pivotal decision.

I was born into a religious family, albeit not Christian. Attendance at Sunday school and church was optional. It wasn't discouraged or encouraged. At our regimented weekly family gatherings, one of the favorite discussion topics, especially among the adult males, was biblical prophecy. The irony was that, to my knowledge, none of my uncles or extended family had attended worship services. But "religious talk" was quite in vogue. On the other hand, I can still see my grandfather draw his ear close to the radio and sense the quieted attention of those present. Over the years, it became like an adult recess during family gatherings when he listened to the Cadle Tabernacle broadcasts.

At the age of thirteen, I suppose I was a typical boy who had been nurtured in that kind of religiously secular environment. My Sunday school attendance was irregular to say the least. I had a respect for and a conscience about the Bible, but my life conformed primarily to the culture around me. But something was beginning to happen that, in retrospect, I understand more fully. The Holy Spirit, through prevenient grace, was consistently nudging me toward the heavenly kingdom, although I did not recognize or acknowledge this at the time. Not many thirteen-year-olds can get their heads around such terms and concepts.

During a vacation Bible school at the small, rural Vans Valley Methodist Church, I made my first effort at being a Christian. I did two things. At the urging of Miss Wilson, an ardent leader of the Women's Christian Temperance Union (WCTU), I signed the pledge: "With God's help, I promise to abstain from all alcoholic beverages." For many of you reading this, the WCTU is likely rather foreign, but during my childhood it was a powerful social movement, largely evangelical, with aims at keeping the nation pure and sober. And its message rattled my cage.

Also, having been presented a Gideon edition of the New Testament, again at Miss Wilson's loving and concerned direction, I signed my name indicating "My Decision to Receive Christ as My Savior." This didn't become the defining date of my life. A key step, but not that transforming of a decision.

Between then and January 26, 1950, I cannot say that either of those commitments were faithfully kept—but I never forgot them.

The Sunday before January 26, my older brother and I were preparing to attend Sunday school at the little Wesleyan Methodist Church in Sunbury,

Ohio, my hometown. My parents did not attend at all, but that Sunday I said, and I cannot remember why, "Mom, why don't you go to Sunday school with us today?"

"I will," she replied, "if you will stay for church." I agreed we would if that was what she wanted.

We had no idea the church was in the middle of a "revival meeting" (that's what we called them in those days) with the evangelistic team of the Reverend and Mrs. Harold Baker, who led the service after Sunday school.

I confess, the service made no impression on me, with no lingering memories. However, unbeknownst to me, at that afternoon's weekly extended-family gathering at my grandparents' farm, Mom told of the "preacher" she had heard that morning. And she proceeded to recount his message. She challenged my father, along with her brother and his wife, to attend the meeting that would be held the next night. They all accepted the challenge and attended on Monday evening.

Later accounts from the pastor, the Rev. Walter W. Jeffries, and the evangelist stated that when they saw my dad enter the church that evening, he was the hardest, toughest-looking man they had ever seen. And yes, they immediately began to pray for him.

The next night, they went to church again—an unprecedented behavior on their part! I did not attend with them either time, though I knew they were going.

When they returned from the Wednesday night service, my mother told my two brothers and me, "Boys, you have a new daddy!" All four of them had, as they would testify, "been saved" that night! When I heard that news, a deep well erupted in my soul. I knew enough to grasp the gravity of the situation. I went immediately to my room and wept.

The following night my "born-again" relatives returned to the revival meeting, and I with them. It was the most miserable, most glorious night of my life. I remembered nothing of that service, I mean nothing—from the time I was seated until the invitation was issued. Later I was told that when I entered the sanctuary, I was seated in the middle of the back pew between my uncle, aunt, and my parents. Somehow, at the time of the invitation, I was at the end of the pew nearest the outside wall of the church; I had no recollection of how or when I had changed positions. They told me that during the service I had exited the sanctuary and returned. In that action I had changed my seating position. I did not know that, but as you will see, it was, I believe, divinely appointed.

After the evangelist's sermon concluded and the invitation hymn was being sung, Pastor Jeffries slipped to my side as I stood on that outside aisle. He asked me if I was a Christian. The first thing to pop into my mind was the signing of that Gideon New Testament in VBS. I responded yes. He, wisely, responded, "You're glad your parents have been saved then, aren't you?"

When he said that, he stepped away, and the inner wells of my being exploded in tears—yet I stood fast. The next thing I knew, a big, lovable bear-of-a-farmer, whose hands were the size of small hams, put his arm around my shoulders and lovingly appealed to this weeping teenager, "Wouldn't you like to let Jesus come into your heart?" Just as quietly, I said yes. With the slightest nudge from his great arm, I was led to the altar, to the Lord, and to what has become a lifetime of being a Christian.

I don't remember what occurred at that altar. Some have said they were there the night I was saved, and they helped to pray for me as I prayed. I take their word for it. It is all a haze to me, except I know that that night, January 26, 1950, in that little white Wesleyan Methodist Church, the heart hunger of a thirteen-year-old boy was satisfied and an entire life was redirected!

When I went home that night, I was new. Lying in bed, reflecting upon what had occurred to and in me, my mind turned (oh, the wonderful manner of God's workings) to my plans to become a radio-television technician. At that time, TV was a fledgling industry, but one with a promising future.

I had already begun collecting literature on technical schools. As I thought of this, I sensed a voice. It was not audible except in my own consciousness: "Why don't you preach for me?" I had not the slightest doubt about, or fear of, that invitation. I immediately answered, "If that's what you want, Lord, it's OK with me." I turned over and immediately went to sleep.

From that day to this, I have never wavered from that call. Never have I wondered if God really had called me into the Christian ministry. I constantly have wondered, "Why me?" A thirteen-year-old kid from a little, obscure farming village in central Ohio. What an adventure it has been!

My intention immediately was transformed from tech school to college. I instinctively knew God's call to preach was a call to prepare for the task. I would be the first of the Glenn family descendants to attend college, and certainly the first to become a preacher.

If I had followed my own plan, my life would never have been as rich as it has become. While there were (and are) times I was so homesick for my hometown, I could hardly stand it, I would not trade my adventure with Christ for anything in the world.

Those two decisions on January 26, 1950, molded my life: to allow Christ to be my Savior and Lord and to follow his call into the Christian ministry. Had I not made those decisions, you would never have heard of Don Glenn except, perhaps, on TV's *America's Most Wanted*, and I am very serious with that declaration. I write these words telling this story only because I knelt before Christ the night of January 26, 1950.

Between then and now has been a life of adventuring with Christ. Because I followed him, I had the wife (now deceased) and have the family I have today. My life has been filled with wonder because my pursuit of Jesus has been filled with pleasant surprises.

This kid from Sunbury, Ohio, would never have dreamed that, in the pursuit of his adventure with Christ, he would travel to every one of the United States, live for extended times in four of them, minister in several foreign countries, and be invited twice to minister before a state legislature.

His high school teachers, back then, would probably be amazed that he would earn a graduate degree, let alone teach university-level courses and be published. Who would have dreamed it? I certainly did not—but I have lived it. I am living it.

My loving Savior has given me fulfillment, satisfaction, and hope. Hope that transcends this earthly life and existence, because of what happened on January 26, 1950, a date that will live in eternity.

LOOKING FOR JESUS

SIA M'BAYO

Editor's Note: We sometimes hear of others' good deeds long before we meet them—even people in our own church. So meet Sia. Her efforts on behalf of the disenfranchised have surfaced in many discussions with my wife and local colleagues. This fall, simultaneous with the editing of this chapter, a group selected her for a major honor—the Tony Maidenberg Award for Community Service. It's Indiana Wesleyan University's top award in this area, granted annually before a gathering of the entire campus. While she doesn't mention it below, the list of her contributions to community efforts for the poor and downtrodden is long and admirable—even among social workers. Perhaps the fact that she doesn't mention such things is itself a major reason for the award selection. Her work among these groups also affords a glimpse of the tandem of praise and worship she discusses in her following reflection. Sia is transparent in how she processes her relationship with God, and, as with all chapters in this collection, her theological views are her own. They prompt us to think "What if?" questions about how we would have tried to process the same situations, and how we would respond to her views if joining her for coffee.

Although my parents found each other through church involvement, their personal struggles resulted in me spending much of my childhood outside the church. My mom was raised Catholic but occasionally attended a Baptist church in Marion, Indiana. My dad was from Sierra Leone. Wesleyan missionaries helped him come to America and attend Marion College (now Indiana Wesleyan University). Ironically, you might say they raised me secular or unchurched.

When they wandered away from the church, it discouraged me from formal religious training. But I knew that God existed and I always wanted to learn more about him. When my friends and I played, they wanted to play school, house, or hospital. I always wanted to play church.

In my childhood, God placed special moments that became religious signposts. The Lakeview Church bus ministry picked me up for a special event when I was ten. I was elated because they said Jesus was going to be there. I would finally get to meet him! After an extended time of fun, they informed us it was time to get back on the bus. But I was sitting at the top of the bleachers in Lakeview's gym, crying. I had counted so much on getting to meet Jesus, and I hadn't seen any sign of him.

Suddenly, it was as if I were sitting in a beam of bright light, and I felt his arms around me—the comfortable, comforting weight of them on my shoulders—and I just knew it was him. It's hard to explain, other than saying I knew him and loved him because he loved me first. That's my first memory of getting to know Jesus: unorthodox, but unforgettably impressed on me as a child. The interaction with Christ continued in unorthodox fashion, only I didn't know it.

Shortly after the Lakeview incident, I started hearing someone calling my name when I was playing or doing homework in my room. It sounded like my parents, so I would run to the other room where they were, to see what they wanted. They always said they hadn't called me and suggested maybe I had imagined it. They would get so frustrated with me. But it kept happening, and I kept wondering what was going on until the day I heard the story of Samuel (see 1 Sam. 3). Then I knew. I was seeking for God, but he was seeking so much harder for me!

In middle school, many of my friends and I couldn't wait for the school day to end. We would dash to our homes and shut ourselves in our rooms. But our rush was prompted by different motives. They hurried to watch TV or finish homework so they could go outside. Not me. I couldn't wait to tell God about my day. I sang songs to him and made up dances. I didn't know it then, but what I was doing was praising and worshiping him.

Somehow, even with these supernatural encounters, I let my desire for God dwindle during my teen years. Boys began to capture my interest. I wanted to be noticed, to be a leader, to be cool. I made some choices that were not the ones God would have made for me. I didn't see it then, but God had given me the ability to lead, along with the ability to assess a situation. If my friends and I were going to go someplace or do something, I was never comfortable unless I had gone there first by myself and surveyed it ahead of time.

God also gave me the ability to fit in with all kinds of people. In high school, I had friends who were head-bangers, "alternative" kids, kids who liked rap music, and others who liked country music. I even had friends whose parents were extremely prejudiced and informed me, "You're the only black person my mom and dad will let in the house." Even then God was preparing me to be able to go into the places where hurting people are—people who are trapped by sin—and lead them out to freedom in Christ.

As I entered my twenties, I wanted a child. I prayed often, asking God for a child. My parents had raised me with basically good morals. I knew not to cheat, lie, and steal, but celibacy and purity until marriage had never come up as a topic. It never crossed my mind to ask for a husband before I asked for a child.

For many of you reading this, if not most, this doesn't seem like something God would bless. I can only surmise that in my ignorance of biblical teaching and any mentorship, I prayed for what I thought were good things. Whether we conclude that God answered my prayer anyway, or that God allowed me to have a child and still love me, I was blessed with my son, Elijah. As life has unfolded, one thing is certain—through Elijah I've come to know God more deeply.

After my son was conceived, everything looked different. Everything. Even my sometimes-difficult relationship with his father. I somehow understood that things weren't as God desired. I remember crying out and confessing to the Lord that I was living a life of sin—that I had forsaken him and allowed my desires to carry me away from him. I apologized for having a child out of wedlock. I did not want Elijah raised not knowing or experiencing God. I wanted to correct my wrong; I wanted to feel Jesus' presence the way I used to! To love him the way I used to. He seemed so far away from me. I just wanted "us" again, and I wanted my family to be churchgoing and God fearing.

I finally realized that I had asked for things out of order. I should have asked for a husband before I asked for a child. I talked with Elijah's father. I told him that our life was out of order. I drew a line: "Either we get married and we find a church or our relationship is over, because I won't continue in sin anymore!" He agreed and we started attending church, but his lifestyle choices proved stronger than his desire to continue to follow Christ. He would go out partying on Thursday nights and not come home until Sunday evening. I wasn't sure: was I more hurt that I would go days without hearing from him or that he turned away from God, as I once had? He started to despise the fact that I prayed and read the Bible in the early mornings and read the Bible to Elijah before bed. Despite turned to hate, and my relationship with Elijah's father became abusive, as it had been early in our relationship.

I stayed out of fear and hope for a better future, and he promised it would never happen again. I knew he loved us the best way he knew, so we continued to plan our wedding. But when Elijah was sixteen months old, and two weeks before we were to marry, his father died in an auto accident. The first responder at the accident told me that he did not die instantly. They had a chance to speak with him. I like to believe that was God's mercy and grace, a chance for him to repent and ask Jesus into his heart.

When Elijah was three years old, he was diagnosed with autism and I became a single mom raising a special-needs child. At times I have wondered if raising a special-needs child alone was meant as a thorn in my flesh, yet in my heart I know Elijah is a blessing.

When I received Elijah's diagnosis, I asked, "God, why?" God reminded me of a conversation we had when I was praying for a child. He had asked me several "what if?" questions, including, "What if I give you a special-needs child to raise?" I had promised him then that I would see even a special-needs child as his gift. I would raise that child to love and serve the Lord.

It was after Elijah's diagnosis that I learned the difference between praise and worship. Praise is when we thank God for his blessings and gifts. It's an outward expression of our inward beliefs. Worship is our inward beliefs of what we outwardly express. It's subduing ourselves before God in all things; for me, it means lifestyle worship. That is, when something (or many things, or everything) is going wrong, we magnify and glorify him anyway. Worship is when we can say, "Lord, I'm so ill. I don't have enough food. I've lost my home. My clothes are worn out, and it seems like my family and friends have abandoned me, but you are still God, and I worship you because of who you are!" Worship is when we look past the gifts—or apparent lack of them—and stand in awe of the Giver. Worship, standing in awe of God, will make you want more of him.

About eight years ago, I felt that there had to be more to life than "eat, sleep, work, repeat," so I earnestly sought God in new ways, including going on a Daniel Fast for twenty-one days. A Daniel Fast involves eating only raw vegetables and drinking only water for a certain period. During my Daniel Fast, God showed me anew my worth in his eyes. He showed me the purpose for which he created me; he told me who I was in him. I began to bear fruit and realize my spiritual gifts in fresh ways. I sensed he was preparing me for the next work he would give me.

Although I still experience times of shaking or pruning, God continues to prepare me for the next step in following him. Psalm 37:4 proclaims, "Delight yourself in the LORD; And He will give you the desires of your heart" (NASB). I'm learning what that verse means; not that God will grant every little desire I have, but that he will plant desires in my heart—for others and myself—things I never would have thought of on my own.

God has recently planted in my heart a craving for more of him, not merely knowledge about him. More than words about him, which are cherished, but a craving for his presence. He is calling me back to my first love, to being that little girl who hurries home to tell him about her day. He is calling me to learn to discern his voice all over again, communicating with me in a new way, as he teaches me the difference between obedience to the rules and submission to the One I love.

He is the Potter and I am the clay. The fact that I'm reaching for him reminds me that he is still reaching for me. My journey has been long, with miles to go before I sleep. But on this homestretch, I'm falling deeper in love with the same God who met me in the Lakeview bleachers.

HANDLE YOUR BUSINESS, GUNS OPTIONAL

ANDREW MORRELL

Editor's Note: This story is written by a friend who looks like he just stepped off a NFL field. His fun and approachable personality seems rather out of sync with his manly physique. But that's Andrew, a lifelong Marion native whose smile can swallow a conversation. I suppose it's no surprise that one of his best friends is the NBA phenom Zach Randolph, his Marion High School classmate. While I know Andrew better than Zach, I had never heard about the incident described below. When you read it, you'll wonder how such a thing would not be familiar to all church members, especially when it occurred to someone who's been sitting among us for decades, a former board member, and founder of the church's longstanding JCBodyshop student ministries' program. I had never heard the story, though I have logged many hours with Andrew's mentor, Charlie Alcock. This story, like so many others in this book, reminds me of the value of every church seeking out stories from its own pews. You'd like Andrew. He runs a construction business, and you'd want to break something on your house just to hire the guy.

I suppose there are real benefits to being born big boned, such as in sports, in running a construction company, and in surviving a gunshot to the face. Only God knows all the details, but listen in and I'll tell you what I know about that night and my subsequent journey. God works in mysterious ways. The Bible says his thoughts are higher than ours, and his ways are not ours (see Isa. 55:8). Well, the following is my firsthand experience with this reality.

I've spent my entire life in Marion, where I was raised by a single mom. Fortunately, I had a great friend in my grandfather. Neither he nor my mom was involved in the church, and so I wasn't either. My grandfather's new relationship with a churchgoing friend changed the frequency of my own church attendance when I was ten. In a sense, it changed my life. I was baptized at the age of twelve and became more involved in church activities, but spiritual growth remained elusive.

Charlie Alcock, a youth pastor with a megaphone voice, seemed to shout into my soul. Deeper spiritual interest that began during occasional visits to outreach activities at Lakeview Wesleyan Church, never really ended. Charlie manifested a magnetic passion for Jesus, exhibited through his exuberant, fun-loving nature. It was infectious. I really wanted to grow in my faith, but our lives went in separate directions with his job changes and my choices. Besides that time with Charlie and my grandfather, my life was largely devoid of male role models.

By the end of high school, I was no longer attending church and the guys I spent time with were just as broken as I was. Though I hadn't lost belief in God, I wasn't doing anything to encourage that belief to mature. In the years that followed, my life at several different schools was tumultuous to say the least. The choices I made were problematic, and the lifestyle I led didn't leave much room for God at all.

But one night changed everything. January 18, 2003, got my attention, and almost took my life. It was another night with my friends at a club.

Ironically, that night I was the sober one. I hadn't been drinking, and when we reached the car I ordered my friend to let me drive. We switched places and I drove. Then, in one of those odd moments that stick with you for life, he looked at me and suddenly commanded, "Drew, duck!"

Instead, I curiously turned my head to look out the driver's-side window. My eyes locked onto a man with a gun aimed at the window as he began firing. Two more men behind the truck began shooting. After the first shot, I flattened on the seat. As soon as I realized the bullets had stopped, I sat up and drove off. I wasn't in pain, but my friend noticed blood on my face, which I attributed to cuts from the glass in the window. But a closer inspection revealed that I had been shot in the face; the bullet had lodged in my neck. Miraculously, I wasn't in pain. A police officer called an ambulance and I remember feeling no worry or anxiety about the situation. As my friend was profusely apologizing and fretting, implying he was the intended target, I remember saying, "It's going to be OK."

After years of ignoring God, I sensed him there that night, and the indifference was gone for life.

At the hospital, the doctors examined the wound, taking X-rays and running tests. The bullet traveled through my face to my neck, missing my jugular vein. I had no broken bones, no lasting injuries, and I left the hospital within a day with instructions to return in a week after the swelling had gone down in my neck, so the bullet could be removed.

I was incredulous. God had spared my life. He certainly didn't have to; I didn't deserve it. But he had. While I was still pondering this, my friend brought an AK-47 to my house, simply telling me, "Handle your business." And I thought about it. But I was still floored by God's mercy. He had just saved my life. What right did I have to take someone else's life when I had just been given such grace? I prayed, asking God to forgive my sins. I prayed for the man who shot me and asked that someday God would let me talk to him when the time was right. For about three years these thoughts dominated me. God had spared my life, but I often felt empty. I was miserable.

Realizing that God was the one who extended me mercy, and that I could—and should—turn to him, I rededicated my life to him in 2006. I had experienced altar calls before, but this rededication was finally real for me, bringing lasting change in my life. It was a renewing of my mind beyond explanation. I began studying the Bible earnestly. Perhaps it's ironic, but I became a disciple of Christ in a rather secular setting, at Starbucks, spending hours there studying my Bible. I was growing in my faith, possibly for the first time. I found men I could model my life after—men who were following God and learning his will, men who had wives and families and were trying to live as God wanted—men whom I wanted to emulate. I was completely open to God and whatever direction he would lead me.

While I prayed for direction in my life, I also prayed for the man who shot me. I got a phone call from a friend in 2008, telling me that he was in the same prison as the shooter and offering to "take care of him" for me (likely, at the least, making his life miserable). But that's not what I wanted. Instead, I asked if I could talk to him. He took the call and I explained who I was. He remembered me. I finally had my chance to talk to this man, and I couldn't do anything less than pass on the grace I had been given. I explained, "I forgive you. I know where you are right now, and it's not over for you. I've given my life to the Lord Jesus Christ. He's forgiven my sins, so how am I not to forgive you? It's not over for you; God wants a relationship with you, too. I will continue to pray for you, brother. God bless." He seemed taken aback by that and said as much to my friend later. God's mercy had protected me, and I was able to tell that man that I hold no bitterness toward him about the past and, by God's grace, could wish him well for the future.

During this time, I was praying for God's direction in my own life for him to make it clear to me. My pastor from the first church I had attended advised me to fast and pray, because he felt God was calling me to something and wanted to reveal it to me. I did so.

God has used several people in my life and all of them had asked me if I felt called to the ministry. That wasn't something God had made abundantly clear to me, so I told them I didn't think so, but I was open to the idea. Shortly after, a significant temptation came my way, and by the grace of God I overcame it. The very next day, my mentor called, and without a word of greeting said, "You're going to be a pastor." After so much prayer, God's call was evident. The question then was what to do next?

Those next steps in my life included enrolling at Indiana Wesleyan University, practicing discipleship, and beginning the process of planting a multicultural church. I have a strong passion for the gospel and for people, and this is God's call on my life.

Years ago, my friend offered me a gun to handle my business, but I realized that the days and years that followed were teaching me to turn to God rather than empty violence. Trusting his mercy and intentionally seeking him led to deeper joy than anything else I've experienced. I'm bi-vocational, serving where God calls me in ministry while having a business. And I see Charlie Alcock regularly. I think his voice is even louder now.

FINDING JOY AGAIN

JOAN (McMANUS) BARDSLEY

Editor's Note: Some people have a stage presence that is all their own. No real comparison. It's just them, one-of-a-kind. That's the wide-smiling, superlative-laden magnetism of Joan. It was no surprise that she was a local Romper Room *TV personality for so many. Long before she became a member of our church, I heard her in public settings, always the consummate children's teacher, and a standard-bearer for educators. In some ways, Joan has lived a simple life. In other ways, it's been sensational. She's known those long dark nights of the soul and the sorrow of losing two special husbands, but she's also been so blessed at times to be slap-happy silly. And she delights in helping others feel the same. Joan is one of those church members who, though petite, is large in influence. She fills any room with joy, regardless of any personal trials.*

▼ ▼ ▼

For many years I was known as Mrs. Romper Room. What a joy. I suppose I retain that persona in viewers' minds to the present. Like one's first-grade teacher, you become a fixed part of their journey, a reference point. And that's been a wonderful distinction.

With my *Romper Room* role came a rather unexpected blessing. As hostess of this children's television program (aired via WPTA, Fort Wayne, ABC), I was invited to speak at a daycare workers' banquet at College Wesleyan Church: a congregation unknown to me before this invitation and located in, what was another unfamiliar setting, Marion, Indiana. God must have been smiling. The very next year, guess where he moved us— from Fort Wayne to Marion, Indiana!

Because of a life-altering physical condition that severely compromised my first husband, Jack, the best we could manage was rather sporadic church attendance. Nonetheless, the College Wesleyan Church family fully embraced us, and, I might add, "As is."

Among the challenges came companions. Deep friends. Accommodating church members. Carol Bence (see pp. 124–128) founded and remained the fulcrum of this group. We named it the Winsome Wesleyan Women's Bible Study Group, and guess where it moved? Yep, into our dining room. For several years, it met at our home every Tuesday evening. We shared prayer requests, studied the Bible, and lifted up one another's families. We created what I call a giant joy spot!

Although my life situation generally prevented me from going to the church, the church came to me. College Wesleyan Church revealed to me a church without walls. If its mission had a home, I knew that one of its rooms was in my heart.

After Jack died, the Holy Spirit used these Tuesday evening meetings to empower me in special ways. I was able to continue to reach out and "move on" in my grief work. At church, Rev. Steve DeNeff challenged me to "dare to dream" again, and his sermons took me deeper into the Word. Dr. Judy Huffman (pastor of congregational care) led soul-coach training classes and prayer retreats that opened up a whole new world for me. As Pastor Judy challenged us, I learned to "listen to God, while listening to others."

Each season of life has its joys and challenges and includes an unknown element: when will that season end? Will this be the last of our sunset years? Three years after Jack's home-going, in the midst of a season of learning to listen to God, something shocking happened!

I was sixty-five and Harold was sixty-eight, but when we met at the College Wesleyan Church watch night service, we both turned into eighth graders! Before long, Dr. Harold Eugene Bardsley, district superintendent of the Wesleyan churches in northern Indiana, asked me to marry him! I may have been the *Romper Room* queen, so to speak, but he certainly was the region's Wesleyan king. He had a long history of leading pastors, caring for members and their churches, investing countless hours into the IWU board planning and functions, and, even more impressive to me, demonstrating consistent conservative values.

The Winsome Bible study group flew into productivity mode. These fun women had an engagement party for us, complete with an original song and poem by Arlene Voorhis, sung by the Bible study group chorus! Six months later, they personally catered our wedding reception, down to the real flower blossoms strewn lavishly over the delectable buffet offerings.

I entered another stretch of life that I thought would take me into eternity, but it, too, had its autumn. Once again I navigated a season when beautiful leaves begin to fade and the stalwart trees are measured in silhouette against the setting sun. After only five and a half years of marriage, in February 2009, the Father called Harold Eugene home. I have no doubt that God greeted him with "Well done, good and faithful servant!" (Matt. 25:21). Pastor DeNeff tenderly and passionately led my husband's memorial service. My "over-the-years friends in Christ" mourned and celebrated with me. To this day, even though the Father has moved me to Atlanta, Georgia, they remain my spiritual cheerleaders and mentors.

I'm now in another season of life and I won't know what to name it until it's over, but once again God is in it.

When we give our whole potential to the Lord, he has a wild and wonderful adventure planned for us. Even before the foundation of the world was laid, God knew us! We are chosen, valued, and forgiven. And for me, College Wesleyan Church has been an instrument of that ongoing transformation.

God has walked with me during all my seasons of life, and will continue to do so: from the Romper Room to the Upper Room.

"Rejoice in the Lord always. I will say it again: Rejoice!" (Phil. 4:4).

RUNNING A DIFFERENT RACE

PAM HALL

Editor's Note: Some stories seem to have clear beginnings and endings, like most in this book. But others reveal an author still writing the storyline, like Pam's story. She remains daily involved in her race and emphasizes hope in things large and small—and for the duration. It's a journey that has taken her from being a local standard for health and beauty, to a woman having a classy but challenged profile with a cane. Although she can't provide the ending bookend of the following story—in essence, the story of her adult life— she affords us a look at themes she has recognized in dealing with crises. She also points to God's attributes that bring hope even now in the midst of them.

▼   ▼   ▼

For a long time, the gym was my personal haven. I loved the challenges that came with pushing my ability to run farther, lift more, and go harder. Exercise had always been what I turned to in good and bad times. It was my comfort zone, the place where achieving my goals and working hard became my identity. As a certified personal trainer, I was thrilled to meet challenges, to help others on their road to health, and to have a degree of control in my life. I could control my health with the right lifestyle and the right amount of hard work. I thought I could fix the problems that arose. Sadly, I didn't always finish my devotions, but I always made time to exercise.

Everything changed on April 20, 2002. It was a beautiful day. After a morning run, I asked my husband, Mark, if we could move the propane tank to make way for the deck we were building. I call Mark my Superman, because he can fix or build just about anything. In the process of moving it, the fluid inside shifted, and the two-thousand-pound tank fell on me, breaking five bones in and around my pelvic area. Instantly my life changed. I needed so much help and I couldn't repair myself. I went from being a fixer, to relying on the assistance of others. I thank God for Mark and my children, our family, our church, and our friends. They supported me the entire time.

With therapy, my recovery progressed well, until my left leg started moving involuntarily and with increasing frequency. After seeing many doctors, I was diagnosed with dystonia, a neurological movement disorder that could progress to my whole body.

I was scared. I was a self-sufficient personal trainer who loved to work hard. My mother later shared her favorite Bible verse with me: "In my distress, I cried unto the LORD, and he heard me" (Ps. 120:1 KJV). I was living that verse. God was always faithful. I cried out to God and he heard my prayer. He met me at my knees. I feared the disorder and its possible outcomes, but in time God gave me the strength to look beyond what might happen and instead remain in the present. Even so, I missed my old self.

Through the next years, my dystonia progressed to my other leg, right arm and shoulder, throat, and neck. With it came odd movements or jerking, as well as vocal, breathing, and swallowing issues. Occasionally I needed a cane, which I hid as best I could. My body took on a mind of its own, which was out of my control. Though I wasn't angry, I felt lost; Who am I? I had been a fixer, personally and professionally focused on meeting rising challenges with hard work, but I could no longer apply those same methods.

The theme of accepting what I could not fix heightened as our family developed a "connection" through different physical disorders. In 2007, my daughter Meagan, suffered with chest pain and was diagnosed with a right bundle branch block in her heart. Her doctor advised me not to hover and unnecessarily restrict her activities, though I so wanted to. In 2008, my other daughter, Mackenzie, developed an osteomyelitis bone infection in her left foot, resulting in emergency surgery. Then in 2009 she was diagnosed with complex regional pain disorder (CRPD or RSD). I have cried countless times watching her suffer through severe pain, knowing that I'm incapable of fixing it, all the while thanking God for leading us to helpful professionals.

In that same year, Mark was diagnosed with vitiligo, which causes the loss of skin pigmentation. In 2010, Meagan was diagnosed with Raynaud's phenomenon, which causes a narrowing of the blood vessels. Also in 2010, Mark and I were in a motorcycle accident. We thank God it was not worse than a totaled bike and some heavy road rash.

During these years, my parents' health was failing and it was hard to not be able to fix it for them. I struggled to be all the things they needed me to be, to accomplish all that my family needed from me, and to live up to all that my work required me to be. All of this took its toll on my family, marriage, work, and health. Internalizing James 4:8, "Draw near to God, and he will draw near to you" (ESV), became a challenge for me. I decided to spend more time seeking God as my refuge and strength.

I needed God's grace more than ever in December 2012. My father died, and about a week later, Mark's father passed away—doubling deep emotional wounds. A month later, after a hysterectomy, I ended up in critical care when the dystonia affected my breathing and exacerbated other erratic movements. When I came home, I needed a walker and my right arm wouldn't be stilled as the disease progressed. In the midst of this, God reminded me of his faithfulness: while Mark maintained his work schedule, friends and extended family members stayed with me, brought in food, sent encouraging cards, prayed for us, and loved us through it all.

Perhaps I was naïve, but I hadn't given up hope of returning to work or regaining my health. I wanted to walk well and be able to care for my family and others; instead, I was the one who needed help. In the fall of 2013, our marriage was barely holding on, our family was hurting, my body was fighting me, and I had to learn a new way to make life work. I knew I often got in the way of God.

In my distress, I cried out to God, and, yes, he heard me. How could God be so patient with me? I told my children, "I do not know how to fix this, but I promise to seek God more every day because I know he is the answer." And he is. There were many four o'clock mornings with God. He is faithful in every situation. Psalm 73:26 says, "My health may fail, and my spirit may grow weak, but God remains the strength of my heart; he is mine forever" (NLT). I began to accept how much I need God. I cannot do this on my own. I am truly weak and he is strong.

The answer is not in having everything "right" today; it is in trusting God for today and tomorrow. I am learning to run a different race, not just with my body, but also with my heart. He has carried me even when I have not let him. I have a long way to go, but I know that God is faithful and he is enough! I thank God for many happy memories, but I am truly thankful for the hard times as well, for I realize those are the times I have grown the closest to God, relying on his strength and not my own.

God has taught me so much in loss and tragedy. He has blessed me with beautiful sunrises, sand between my toes, my family's laughter, walks, coffee, smiles from strangers, love from family, church, and friends. There is much more peace at home now. I love Mark in a deeper way, and am so thankful for our family—Courtney, Tristan, Meagan, and Mackenzie.

Although I can no longer provide hands-on personal training, God has opened doors for me to start a small business with excellent certified personal trainers. I feel a closeness to God in a way I didn't realize was possible, newly appreciative of his perpetual presence, unconditional love and forgiveness, patience, and complete sovereignty. And, he still gives me the hope and energy to strive to put my cane aside one day.

Hebrews 13:8 says, "Jesus Christ is the same yesterday and today and forever" (ESV). He remains the same, always good and always faithful. It is me he is changing through all of these circumstances. Romans 15:13 says, "May the God of hope fill you with all joy and peace as you trust in him, so that you may overflow with hope by the power of the Holy Spirit." From distress to peace, God has always heard me, and he patiently continues to teach me how to live a new life in him.

THROUGH THE FIRE

STEVE JACKSON

Editor's Note: *I'm now getting a close look at retirement decisions. At fifty-seven-years old, I have peers making key decisions for life's after-work season. My brother retired at age forty-five. My grandfather retired twice then worked nearly full-time sacking groceries into his nineties. My friend Harry is in his seventies and seems fit enough to work another thirty years. (He just hiked the twenty-three-mile ridge route at the Grand Canyon.) My friend Jeanne retired many years ago from the science laboratories at Indiana Wesleyan University and then took on a major part-time role, a dream job of sorts, working on the college's grounds crew, maintaining the plants. Retirement is a funny thing. In some ways complex, in others, rather simple. My friend Tom is nearly eighty and just started another pharmaceutical company in the 3D printing sphere. Another friend, about the same vintage, Wilbur, seems to have many jobs and still teaches college courses and takes large groups overseas. While some things are certain, others are not. For example, what will our quality of life be in retirement? That's what Steve wrestles with below. It's really not how old we are when we cross that retirement threshold, but how old we feel. And then there's our level of fulfillment as we face each new day.*

Retirement. After thirty-four years at the fire department, I had arrived at retirement's door. But the looming question wasn't, what do I want to do first? Rather, I wondered how I could serve God now that I wasn't working in that capacity. My life calling had been at the fire department, and I felt God's presence there. Contentment abounded. He saw me through everything. Quite literally, he brought me through the fire. Because he was with me, I was never afraid and I remained fully involved in my duties until the day I retired. The old saying proved true, "Wherever you are, be there until you leave" (see Mark 6:10). My heart was there and my vocational journey was as blissful as I could desire. I'm not rich in funds, but I sure am in memories. I loved working there.

Walking out of the station for the last time as an employee took me down unfamiliar streets—the future without employment.

Initially, you could have found me aimlessly wandering along those post-employment paths. I plodded through some tough terrain of discontent and disconnection, since so much of my joy had come from serving God at the fire station. What did he want me to do next? It was a question I asked daily. Imagine engaging in a treasure hunt with no map; that's the image I would have fit into. It complicated things—not having a clue of my target destination and not sensing God placing any new opportunities in my life. Nothing. No hints. I might as well have been on the proverbial hamster wheel. In retrospect, it's amazing to realize that God always places us where he wants us, even if it takes us a while to understand it. Hindsight is not always 20/20, but in this case it brought his will into view more clearly.

Prior to my retirement, my mother had passed away after battling cancer. My father did not make a good widower and understandably was lonely. Three months later, he suffered a cerebral stroke but continued living alone.

A month after I retired, he lost the ability to drive and express himself, a change which required a lot more of my time.

Caring for my dad became my best way of serving God, but I didn't see it right away. This care involved taking him to breakfast and eating supper with him, spending time with him, and making sure his needs were met. I hadn't considered it to be serving God, but it was.

It's so easy to worry about being placed somewhere. We quickly wonder what we should be doing for God; we try to identify his specific calling for us. But sometimes, like in my case, his will is right in front of us. It can involve doing something we hadn't previously considered to be "service" and sometimes we may not even realize that we're playing a role in his kingdom and our local community.

If the saying is true that the only things that last forever are God's Word and God's people, I suppose we have an easy gauge to help us determine the value of our commitments. And I suppose that since he's shown me my new role with my father, I may not be fulfilled if I returned to putting out fires.

NEVER TOO OLD TO SERVE

ELAINE NEWTON

Editor's Note: *Throughout this book we've read some rather remarkable stories hidden in the pews all around us. Every church has these stories. Oh, they'll have different names and details, and perhaps different responses and results, but they are common threads in this shared story of humanity. The death of loved ones. Divorce. Physical trauma. Debt. Illness. Despair. Miracles. Fulfillment. Provisions. The list is long. The long list, at least in North America and parts of Europe, includes a season called retirement.*

In the following story, Elaine Newton allows us to glimpse her quiet fulfillment during retirement, as she finds herself in service to an older generation. I've often observed some of my church friends leaving the church in order to go to local nursing homes to lead onsite worship services or Bible studies. Some, like the former dean of students at our local university, have done this for more than twenty years. Although nursing homes may be out-of-sight for a large section of the population, my colleagues find there a community of believers eager for spiritual connections and many others needing to hear of eternal hope in Christ. Even if you do not feel called to help in this particular ministry, Elaine's reflections cross over into other fields of service. After all, retirement is a time when, if we allow God to move in our lives, we can indeed come to a mature level of faith and service.

▼   ▼   ▼

My prayer as a young Christian was, "Father, I want to bring glory to your name." However, I'm not sure if I succeeded in that endeavor during much of my health-care career. In nursing evaluations, I was told to use my head instead of my feet; in other words, be efficient. And professionally I was. I'm afraid my competitive spirit dominated my profile, including my goals and behavior. Though my underlying hope was to please God, in many cases that goal seemed to take a backseat.

In retirement, the honorable aim reemerged. A sense of fulfillment arose when God used my sister and me in a nursing home Bible study. Once again I prayed often, "Father, I want to bring glory to your name."

For several years, we have worked with a group of nursing home residents and have seen firsthand God's amazing work in their lives, and in ours. We shouldn't be surprised that when the supernatural works among the natural, miracles take place.

One rather eccentric woman (we will call her Connie) in the group had great difficulty communicating with others. To put it mildly, she dominated discussions. Concerned that she would bring discord to our group, we prayed, "If she is going to bring trouble, God, please make her go away. Or, if there is a lesson for us, lead on."

God taught us that lesson rather quickly.

We began showing Connie some attention. We listened to her story. We gained insight into who she was and what made her tick, what she'd suffered and what motivated her. We helped her identify why people sometimes reacted to her negatively. In a miraculous way, God made it possible for her to attend a retreat, where she heard a testimony that changed her life. She realized anew that God loves her in spite of her hurts and bitterness. We saw her blossom in her interactions. If her old habits surfaced, a quiet reminder did the trick: "long story short."

Another gentleman (let's call him John) asked us to pray that he would be able to go home by Christmas. It's a reasonable and honorable request, but God had other plans. John has now spent several Christmas seasons in the nursing home and more contentedly sees how God is using him to minister to the staff and other patients. We're also able to laugh a bit at his ability as a lifelong Baptist to accept others' views in the group, especially those from Nazarene backgrounds. Now a leader of the group, he's lowered his denominational boundaries. He's also become our dear friend, though his ability to quote Scripture puts us to shame.

John recently demonstrated compassion for his caregivers when they were unable to put him in his wheelchair to attend Bible study. He has been known to have difficulty accepting such delays in his care. But God has helped him show more concern for a suffering caregiver than his own desires.

Another of our members (let's call her June) recently began giving money to a food bank. June grew up in The Great Depression with parents who had a healthy pride in providing for their family without expecting help from others. They grew a garden and cleaned houses. Her mother made clothes for her children by redesigning clothing from others. The children gathered dandelion greens, strawberries, and even coal along the railroad track to provide for their needs. Those children all grew up as independent individuals and didn't want help from others.

Against this backdrop, it's understandable that June valued the ability to be self-sufficient. But when God told her to give to the hungry, she obeyed, contributing quietly, without fanfare. She simply remarked, "When God tells you to do something, you do it."

Another woman has a son who's been disillusioned with the church since childhood. Its rules did not make any sense to him. Through the love and care he has seen his mother receive, he is realizing that people can love and accept his mother, even when she can be rather dogmatic.

Christian love demonstrated for her, and at times for himself, has opened up his heart a bit.

An assortment of other stories could be added, such as a man who attended the studies for a while, then disappeared. He has since returned, testifying that he gave his heart to God.

Through leading this study, I've been reminded that consistency itself reveals a caring spirit; it also helps us (or any leaders of such groups) to learn behavioral patterns and calculate helpful responses. For example, our simple practice of providing treats influenced one woman's choices. She navigates her schedule and hallways to attend each week—mainly for the desserts. But she also stays and listens to the Bible lesson. For her, and we suppose for a few others, these simple ephemeral treats seem linked to their chances for a taste of heaven.

Through all of this, perhaps the biggest change has been in me. When we let God use us, he changes us. Through this experience, my desire for the Scriptures has increased. After decades of hearing sermons, I'm finally listening to them. They speak into my life and soul. Although I always try to be efficient in my comings and goings, and especially when I take on any project, efficiency is not my overriding passion. It's a means to an end—and that target is pleasing God.

My prayer is that God will help me to reflect his light into the world around me.

PART 8

THE **TRUTH**
OF **OBEDIENCE**
TO **GOD**

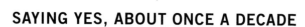

SAYING YES, ABOUT ONCE A DECADE

JUDY (HUFFMAN) CROSSMAN

Editor's Note: Until a few years ago, Judy (Huffman) Crossman seemed to manifest a vocational enigma. She was in her mid-fifties, a longtime friend, very successful, attractive inside and out, and single. The latter was certainly fine, but it wasn't her preference, and not at all what she prayed for. She talked about it, with humor. She never missed segues to discuss singleness. When she recently married a College Wesleyan Church widower, the brilliant artist Rod Crossman, there was dancing in the streets. Well, as much as could be expected by Wesleyans.

When I saw her title for this chapter with the words, Saying Yes, I just assumed I would be editing a piece on that recent nuptial bliss. After all, it was a grand occasion with openly expressed joy by both—and as central to the positive side of a church community as one could witness. But as her story below unfolds, it seems to be about everything except her wedding. Rather, and here's the punch, it's about an obedience that led up to that wedding, a journey that God orchestrated for decades to have her in place to walk that aisle, at that time. There were ministries for her during her long singleness season, as well as now in partnership with Rod. Oh, she doesn't spell it out below, but when you get to the end, it's an obvious deduction.

One day while Judy was dean at Indiana Wesleyan University, she and I paused and reflected on Keith Drury's then new book titled The Call of a Lifetime *(WPH). We've both kept early work schedules for most of our lives, and occasionally we would chat awhile before the rest of the city stirred; our offices were in the same hallway. Keith has had a profound impact on many, including us, and he thrives in the space of practical theology. Judy had just announced that she would be leaving the deanship for a pastoral role across the campus at College Wesleyan Church. I paused and said, "If we had read a book with that title thirty years earlier, you would have never become a dean for a season and I wouldn't have been a youth pastor." In spite of our best efforts and attempts at service, the overriding theme is just that, sincere attempts at obedience. And, by implication, how to discern if answering "no" is actually an option in such a pursuit.*

▼　▼　▼

Sometimes saying yes to God requires making minimal adjustments. Other times, the changes are momentous. If I graphed my lifetime vocational chart, it would look like a ZZ Top lightning bolt, zigzagging with prominent redirections.

In full disclosure, at times saying yes hasn't been easy, even in the smallest of things. God's invitations may come in little promptings, like "Stop and help that older woman find her lost car in this massive parking lot." And sometimes the prompting is bigger, like "Go to Sierra Leone and be a missionary!" In either type of communication, I struggle to know if it is really God or just my imagination. And often the "yes" comes slowly, because it likely means altering my life, and that scares me.

Four key invitations framed my life, and perhaps sharing the process of how I responded to them may be helpful. These are only four in a long stream, but they best represent life-changing discussions with God. They felt huge at the time, and reflection magnifies this perception. In retrospect, God's willingness to communicate with me during those seasons of my life overwhelms me. I'm also a little surprised that I paid enough attention to hear his voice.

Before walking through these four intersections, it's necessary for me to note five people whom I believe God orchestrated to be, what I call, "God translators." They taught me to pay attention to God's voice. They all encouraged me to trust him and to say yes to his invitations.

My parents were my greatest God translators. They were wonderful, loving people who taught us kids to laugh, work hard, and love God and others. They almost always had family devotions. From my birth until their passing, to be with them was to be in God's presence. My mom died at the age of ninety-four in my home, and with her prompting we had daily devotions whenever we were together. Her persistence poured God's presence into my mind like sweet perfume. It familiarized me with God's voice because these daily sessions invited me into his presence.

The next two translators were my grandmothers. They were true prayer warriors. Their approaches to faith differed greatly. Grandma H's provisions came with much outward talk about God and strong calls for me to be holy. Grandma D just lived out her faith joyfully for me to see. But both women prayed for me daily, whether I was with them or not. I will never know the protection that was placed over me through their intercession.

I also need to credit the advice of Mrs. Kenworthy, my pastor's wife for twenty-plus years. You might say I was an "altar runner." Every time there was an altar call, I was there. As the years passed, I eventually cried out to Mrs. Kenworthy, "Why am I the only one who comes up here? Am I that bad? Is everyone else perfect?" And she wisely said, "Keep listening to God. And, Judy, if he asks you to come meet him here, just do it. Keep your heart sensitive to the promptings of the Holy Spirit." She didn't talk to me about anyone else's response; she just encouraged me to develop an inner ear for loving invitations from God. Wow! What wonderful teaching. She didn't speak for God; she encouraged me to learn to listen on my own.

Against this backdrop of saints showing God to me, it seems as if it should be easy to hear from him, to discern that it is truly God speaking, and to say yes eagerly. But as each divine invitation has come, I've struggled.

INVITATION ONE: Marion College 1972, Eighteen Years Old

As a college freshman majoring in elementary education, I sought clarity on my calling during spiritual emphasis week (an intense time of twice-daily sermons). About midweek, I was on sermon overload and sought serenity in my dorm's second-floor chapel. There in that plain Shatford Hall space, it was just God and me, and I told him I was willing to major in anything that he wanted, but I needed some assurance on direction. After a long prayer, I noticed a Bible and opened it to Matthew 9:37–38: "The harvest is plentiful, but the laborers are few . . . pray earnestly to the Lord of the harvest to send out laborers into his harvest" (EJV).

That was a sobering moment, because I recalled Mrs. Kenworthy's lesson on this passage during high school: "Never pray that prayer unless you are willing to be a laborer." God's voice rang clear and such a direct word proved humbling. But moments later the struggle began anew. Thinking that perhaps opening to that Scripture was just coincidence, I turned to God again and said, "If this is really from you, Holy Father, please give me another promise. I mean, if you are in this, surely you can do it again just so I'll be sure I'm hearing from you."

I grabbed another section of pages in the Bible, looked down, and again there was the very same passage, only this time from the Synoptic account found in Luke. You could have hit me with a wet beanbag and I wouldn't have been more stunned. God must have been speaking. But moments passed, and I looked to him again and said, "Father, I believe, but I'm still afraid that I may be making this happen somehow. God, I've got to know that this is you. Please, could you give me one more indication that this is you and not me?" With some hope and some doubt, I reached over and pulled a card out of a stack of small cardboard memory verses set in that once-common plastic "loaf of bread" gizmo.

You guessed it; the one verse I pulled out was Matthew 9:37. Perhaps this sounds ridiculous, or offensive, or is incongruent with your theology. For me, however, as an eighteen-year-old, I met the God of creation in that room and he spoke to me. I later learned that what I did was prostrate myself before God—the same verb used here for worship, which involves kissing the ground. I figuratively put my face to the ground and cried out my utter praise and thankfulness to God for his willingness to speak with me. His invitation was not a call to a new major, but to live as one of his laborers. I spent my college days eager to love God well and to share his love with others. I had heard from God and I wanted to know him better.

INVITATION TWO: Wesleyan World Missions 1977, Twenty-Three Years Old

During my senior year in college, I started applying for teaching positions. No one wanted me. The week before graduation, yet another school had turned me down, so I accepted a job offer as an admissions counselor at Marion College (now Indiana Wesleyan University). Throughout that year I developed a growing sense that I would spend my life differently than teaching in white middle-class America. I didn't know what that meant, but my soul was stirring. I understood that the restlessness was from God, but its meaning remained elusive.

Then August came. In a way, we all need an August meeting in which some key spiritual leader walks into our lives. For me, it occurred during a summer camp where I served as part of my admission's role. My brother's friend began to answer some of my questions with magnetic clarity. The conversation left me with renewed hope in finding vocational peace, and I couldn't shake the discourse. It replayed often over the following days and weeks. But it was that first day that changed the path of my life, especially for the next three years.

This man was Don Bray, and little did I know, he was the new director of personnel for Wesleyan World Missions. That same day he learned of a crisis need for an elementary school teacher. A medical emergency left a boarding school without a teacher. They needed a teacher now! Don found me and said, "This is it! God has been getting you ready for this moment!" Of course it was overwhelming.

My God translators had taught me to bathe such moments in prayer and Scripture. I went down to a quiet ball diamond and told God I was willing to obey. Once again, I asked for his confirmation. I read and prayed; prayed and read. As it began to rain, I asked, "God, I'm not leaving this spot until I hear something from you." So I leaned over my Bible to keep it dry and continued to seek. While I read 2 Corinthians, God spoke. The word he gave me in the little chapel at age eighteen was now being refined. The call to be his laborer now specifically became an invitation to be his ambassador. I was given a ministry of care and reconciliation, though I didn't know any details of that call.

With great confidence and courage, I concurred with Don's perception of God's call and I asked for the details. The need was in Sierra Leone, West Africa, for teaching three grades simultaneously, with a three-year commitment. Oh, and I would need to leave within a month.

Confidence and courage flew out the window. I was twenty-one and terrified and had a weekend to pray about it. It seemed too hard, too far, too much, too fast. I told God that I wanted to be willing, but I wasn't. I pleaded with him to make me willing. I asked him to help me say yes. Two days later the phone call came. They offered a one-year appointment. Later I could choose if I wanted to extend for two more years. This was God's provision! I could say yes to that. God knew my limitations and fears, and he lovingly worked within that. One month later, I was onsite. One year later, I accepted the extended call. Three years later, I completed my days as his ambassador in Sierra Leone.

INVITATION THREE: Urbana 1981, Twenty-Eight Years Old

Upon return I became the personnel supervisor for Wesleyan World Missions (WWM) and loved it! My work took me to a youth conference in Urbana, Illinois, and once again I found myself running to the altar. The call was actually for teens to accept God's call to full-time Christian service. Scores of them, filled with joy and hope, headed down to the front. With utter disgust and near anger, I felt myself getting out of my seat and joining them. As they sang, lit candles, and rejoiced, I slapped my silly armband on the altar (as requested) indicating that I had heard God's latest invitation. Then I slipped out.

A friend found me and asked what was happening. I told him that God was asking for three things from me. First, I sensed God directing me to go on to graduate school. Next, he asked if I was willing to serve him in fairly male-dominated roles. And finally, he asked me to stay single in his service for a long time. All three of those things were very costly for me. I didn't want to leave what I was doing. I was not eager to be in positions that were sometimes threatening to others. And I wanted to be married— now! My answer to God came over the next three months, and it was what felt like a long season of dying to my own hopes and dreams.

God was asking me to step out in faith into situations that had no attraction to me. After days of struggling with God, much like before, I finally asked him to make me willing to be obedient. And he helped me say yes. So I set out on a nineteen-year journey. Hundreds of decisions were made during that season. Sometimes I eagerly obeyed, and sometimes I didn't. But God never left my side; time and again, he led in ways I would not have dreamed of on my own.

INVITATION FOUR: College Wesleyan Church 2005, Fifty-One Years Old

Long after graduate work was behind me, I became the academic dean for Indiana Wesleyan University. Though I was still single and had passed on chances for relationships, I was rather content in my life with Christ. The call from God that had seemed so costly, had resulted in much more good than I could have imagined. My life was full of family, friends, meaningful work, and travel. Then he did it again, but this time it was different on two accounts.

Instead of running to the altar, we settled it in the pew. I sat on the front left seat in the back half of the new College Wesleyan Church. Pastor Steve DeNeff was giving a short sermon before a business meeting. In the middle of this sermon, God spoke to me as clearly as he ever had. It still was not an audible voice, but my whole being knew that God was inviting me into the ministry. He was calling me to leave the University and become a minister of his gospel. And the second difference was how this invitation was wrapped, not in a hue of fear and sacrifice, but with ribbons of joy and peace. This time, the call didn't feel like a hardship, but a true gift. Obedience demanded significant life changes, but I found myself doing what I'd been preparing for my whole life!

I don't know what lies ahead, but I do know that God can be trusted. I know that his invitations will come in ways that surprise me. I know that they are always embedded in goodness for me and for those whose lives touch mine. I pray that all the days of my life I will say yes. I pray that he will be glorified through my obedience.

And perhaps a postscript is in order. In my world, everyone knows the most recent yes. But for those of you reading my story from other states and countries, you might want to buckle in. Yes, I got married at the age of fifty-nine! It's the best gift so far.

LORD, DID I HEAR YOU RIGHT?

SARAH HARRIMAN

Editor's Note: *It's easy to observe a gifted leader and think there was an obvious path to their place of prominence. Often, however, it's inspiring to learn of faith decisions early in their lives that helped form, not only their character, but also forge their career. What Sarah doesn't mention below is that the return to World Gospel Mission, which she shares only in passing, was for her husband to serve as its president. As you read this story, you're left wondering what if they had ignored or excused away God's leading when a promising and higher-paying opportunity arose. We'll never know, but we do have the account of what transpired when they listened and obeyed.*

▼   ▼   ▼

We were still newlyweds when World Gospel Mission asked us to fill in for missionaries in Argentina during their yearlong furlough. With one year of marriage behind us, and with my husband fluent in Spanish, we accepted and helped sustain a newly founded church and youth work.

During our time in the beautiful city of Salta (1975–1976), we sought the Lord's will for our next position. We received several invitations to pastor US churches, and one seemed to linger in our thoughts. The church of about seventy-five to a hundred members was in the small town of Ligonier in northern Indiana. We prayerfully postponed the decision until we could return to the States for a personal visit.

When we met them, we loved the people and felt God wanted to use us there; we also privately thought we'd be there for two years. We just assumed we would return to international ministry, because pastoring long-term was never my husband's desire. I wonder if God just smiled when he heard our thoughts.

Three years later, after some encouraging as well as discouraging times, a district superintendent in Oregon offered us a church twice the size of our Indiana congregation and double the salary. I had grown up in the beautiful state of Oregon and dreamed of returning someday. This was the perfect chance, a "step up," so to speak. For someone who had grown up in the Northwest, the mountains are a whole lot more beautiful than cornfields. When my husband asked us to start packing, it struck me: although it seemed such a simple choice, we really hadn't prayed about it. That's when we individually and collectively committed the opportunity to prayer in earnest.

By the second day, in my regular devotional Scripture reading, I read the parable of the owner of an orchard who had a fig tree that had not produced in three years (Luke 13). It didn't escape me that it was the same amount of time we had served at the church. The owner of the orchard ordered his worker to cut it down, so it would not continue to waste the soil. The worker asked if he could dig around it, fertilize it, and try one more year to promote growth. The owner agreed, the worker did his part, and the fourth year the tree produced figs beyond expectation. That scriptural passage pierced straight to my heart. I knew it was God's word to me. We were to stay right there, dig around the "tree," work with it, and fertilize it.

I didn't say anything to my husband right then; rather, I asked the Lord to somehow speak to him. Later the very same day, he came home from his office to discuss what the Lord had said to him—from Luke 13. Considering our unity, there was just no doubt and therefore no further discussion: we were to stay right there for at least another year.

During that year the Lord blessed the digging, working, and fertilizing, bringing in a record number of new people. Most of these were converts who grew along with us, all of us coming to know God in a special way. Twenty-six years and two building additions later, we were still there, very comfortable with a healthy congregation full of wonderful people. They had become our dear friends. God had more than blessed us. We raised our three precious daughters there, and life was beautiful even without mountains.

In the midst of all that comfort and fulfillment, God gently began to nudge us toward something else, though we didn't know what (another story in itself). His providential leading brought us in 2002 to our ministry with World Gospel Mission.[1]

God has spoken to me many other times through his Word, giving direction, encouragement, confirmation, instruction, and correction. What a precious gift! One very special passage given to me during a time of real soul searching and uncertainty is Psalm 32:8: "I will instruct you and teach you in the way you should go; I will counsel you with my loving eye on you."

I cling to that and go to the Lord with that promise over and over. He never fails to do just what he has promised.

NOTE

1. Her husband, Dr. Hubert Harriman retired as president of World Gospel Mission in July 2016.

A SLOW SHIFT IS STILL A SHIFT

SYDNEY GARNER

Editor's Note: Sometimes an author sets out to tell a lesson learned and does so with confidence. Sydney does this below. This story is classic Sydney— task oriented. Enjoyable and likely written in a large, underlined font. If you knew her, you'd smile, because she's indeed a take-charge woman. If you were starting a new business and needed an intelligent, funny, self-effacing hard worker, that's Sydney. And she seems to like the tough jobs. I work with her husband on some publishing projects, and one day he had to cancel a meeting to drive several states away to pick up Sydney. She had fallen from a ladder while helping her elderly mother and had broken both elbows. Of course I felt sorry for her injury, but I also had to smile, thinking that she likely had tools in both hands and thus the double injury. Every church needs a Sydney. Someone who is vocationally successful, is refreshingly candid about personal shortcomings, and can tell the truth with a smile—whether you want to hear it or not.

▼   ▼   ▼

Before heading out to decorate Christmas trees at the church, I prayed, "Lord, don't let me get so busy that I forget about people." I am task oriented with sights only on the finished project, and I prefer to work alone. This strategy minimizes interruptions.

As I entered the church, I learned that the staff would be off site for the day, with only one volunteer manning the office—perfect. A second volunteer was coming to help me; I briefly entertained putting her to work on the chapel tree while I decorated in the atrium. The Holy Spirit spoke very loudly to my stubborn spirit, "Don't get so busy that you forget about people."

The staff finally left, and my fellow volunteer arrived. She decorated from below while I zoomed up in the lift, doing my own thing. I am not a born conversationalist, but the Spirit kept a steady mantra: "It's about people, not about the tree." This stranger and I chatted a bit. She was a good worker and could talk and work at the same time; God had sent the right person.

The conversation was hit-and-miss, but I was trying. We were both focusing on the task, until God turned my head to notice another woman milling around, watching us. I ignored her for a spell; then I got "the nudge." It was gentler, from inside, but noticeable. It made my mouth move without too much effort: "Hey, would you like to help us?" Now there were three.

We were just three women randomly talking about our lives, but God was determined to remove me from my high horse. Six hands made the tree trimming go faster, but I still felt relieved that now, with the two women working below, I could focus on my task and exit the conversation.

I continued to work, going up and down on the lift, when someone began knocking on the door near the café. We all three stopped, looked, and momentarily froze. I thought if we didn't respond, he might go away, but the Holy Spirit must have employed the other two women that day. While I was still pondering, I heard a voice questioning from below, "Should I let him in?" Both women were looking up at me.

"No, I'll do it," I said, as I came down from my imitation throne. We all knew that there were only four women in the building, three of us over sixty (one was the receptionist). They watched as I opened the door just a few inches to speak to the man, probably in his forties, dragging a suitcase behind him.

Me: "Can I help you?"

Him: "Is there a pastor here that I can talk to?"

Me: "I'm sorry but the whole staff is out of the building today." Maybe he would get the hint.

Him: "You mean there is nobody I can talk to?" He started to cry.

Now everyone has had those short seconds when your mind races and it seems you are spending hours debating. The worldly part of my mind was screaming, "You don't know this man. He might be danger-ous! He just wants money. You don't have time for this. What can you really do for him? If you stop, you won't get the tree done. The tree! The tree! The tree!"

"You can talk to me." The Spirit had done a strange thing to my voice and mind and I opened the door to him. The other two women watched as we moved to the hospitality room, where he told me his story.

He had moved to Marion to be with a woman who had kicked him out many times during their six-month relationship. Supposedly she had addictions, and he had tried to help her but now he had had it. He was try-ing to get to Indianapolis, where his family lived, for the holidays. He had no money, no car, and was only requesting a ride. More tears flowed from this distraught stranger with a worn suitcase.

I told him to relax in the room while I tried to get him some help. Returning to the questioning faces of my volunteers, I gave them a brief synopsis. My first instinct was to say, "Where is a pastor when you need one?" But instead I prayed, "OK, God, whom can I call?"

God answered right away, "Jack Brady."

I did not have Jack in my lists of contacts, so I hurried to the office and asked the receptionist to look up his number. Looking frazzled, she said the computer wasn't working. Without a number, I headed back down the hall, hesitant to leave the man alone for very long.

The Spirit is strong within us if we will listen: "You know Jack works at Indiana Wesleyan University, and you know the generic format of their email addresses."

"Thanks, God." And I sent the email, hoping that Jack would respond. He did—within seconds: "Who is this?" I emailed back my name. Jack replied, "Call me at this number." I related what I knew of the man, and Jack spoke with him on the phone.

The stranger approached, all smiles. "I know this man," he said as he handed me the phone. "He wants to talk to you." Jack informed me that he was on his way over. I hung up. The man was still standing there, smiling. "I know that man," he repeated. "He used to be the chaplain at the jail." He headed back to the hospitality room and I followed. Thrilled that he knew the person coming to help him, he contentedly took a chair. In minutes Jack arrived and took over responsibility for our guest.

I returned to my task, the tree, newly appreciative of the Holy Spirit's patience with me.

It couldn't have been ten minutes before a little elderly man knocked at the door. "What now?" I asked silently, looking up. "It's about people," came the reply, and down I came. I hesitantly opened the door.

Me: "May I help you?"

Him: "I'm from the Salvation Army and I am supposed to pick up some boxes."

Me: "No one is here today, and I don't know anything about that."

Him: "They told me they were in the library."

Me: "OK, let's look."

I sounded more upbeat than I felt. I let him in, unafraid. After all, I was pretty sure I could "take him," since he was older, shorter, and weighed less than I did.

In the library, sure enough, we found packed boxes. The two fellow tree decorators had heard the request, followed unsolicited, and we proceeded to help. But none of us could lift the large boxes, packed with canned goods. One of the women hurried to the kitchen to get a cart, and after much struggling, we had the boxes in his truck. It was cold outside; the boxes were heavy and awkward, yet both women without hesitation or complaining did what it took. These two women were teaching me how to have a helpful, willing spirit, to do anything that needed to be done, even if I thought it was an inconvenience.

When the door closed behind him, I said silently, "OK, Lord, I really would like to get this tree done today, but it is your tree." I wasn't quite ready to wholeheartedly say, "Your work is my work," but my soul was shifting.

Around that time, Jack and the man came out of the hospitality room and headed toward the door. "I'm taking him with me." Jack paused and whispered to me, "I was working on my dissertation." I apologized for the interruption. He cut me off, "No, no, I would so much rather be doing this. This is what it's about." How could Jack think that being interrupted, listening to this man, and using his valuable time to help was fun? Thanks, God, and thanks, Jack, for showing me the true spirit of giving. A little more soul shifting was occurring.

As I climbed back into the lift, the Spirit within turned my head to watch the two men: Jack leading and the other one almost skipping like a young boy following his dad—with faith that everything would be all right. And it was! Jack found him a ride.

"God, please stop me from getting so focused on the moment that I forget about people. And thank you for people like Jack who are never too busy."

The women left. The tree was decorated. But as I sat on the floor assessing our work, I noticed it was slightly askew. My first reaction was to think, *Oh, no. All that work, and now it is leaning a little.*

The tree never stood perfectly straight that year, but now I know it was a way to remind me that my soul shifts slowly and only stands straight when I listen and obey the Spirit within me; otherwise, I'm tilted.

SUNRISE IN THE SUNSET
GOD'S SPECIAL CALL

JAN (HARRISON) TUIN

Editor's Note: When people have boundless energy in their senior years, we want to know their stories. What is the source of this passion? Where did this story begin? What lessons has God taught you? Why bother to tell it? Some of these answers surface below. Jan Tuin leans into her story. A life that begins with rough sledding, ends with some real promise—goodness that will long outlive her and her husband, Lon. Although the Tuin family grew up elsewhere, Jan and Lon moved to Marion, Indiana, to be near their daughters and grandchildren. One of their two daughters is married to Ron Mazellan (see pp. 129–132). The other daughter, Ronda, moved with her family to Marion for the same reason as her parents—to be with family. It's hard to think of our church without this extended family and its various manifestations.

Although I was aware of some of Jan's journey through her published book, I've often found it difficult to think of her in any light other than as being happy. There's a skip in her step, explained in the story below. Regardless of sins against us, in her case, relentless childhood abuse, God has a purpose for our lives and can fuel the passion to pursue that vision. While we normally don't wait until our seventies to give first-rate priority to first-rate causes of our calling, sometimes it works this way.

I hope this telling of her story doesn't lose the value I see—that the earlier decades of her life were rich with ministry to the community and her family— now paying dividends in and for the younger generation. Unlike President Reagan's statement, she's not riding off into the sunset of life. Instead, she understands this season of her life as being filled with sunsets and sunrises. She sees the hopeful dawn of each new day.

▼　▼　▼

When my mother died of cancer at the age of thirty-four, I felt like a part of me also died. I was eleven years old, and my life forever changed. My dad remarried six months later, and my stepmother seemed to hate me. Hardly a day passed when she did not remind me that I was worthless and would never amount to anything.

She often made negative comments about my mother, hitting hard that she was "no good." She seemed deeply jealous of my mother and her memory. People in our church dearly loved my mother and often told me how much I looked like her. For this young girl, any comparison to my mother became the perfect opportunity for my stepmother's condescending treatment.

The daily cycle of verbal and emotional abuse was relentless. In the evening, I would retreat to my special hideaway to be with God. I felt safe there, next to the ditch bank in the middle of our orange grove in Anaheim, California. I soaked in the scenes of God's hand brushing vivid strokes of color across the sky, creating magnificent sunsets. His creation assured me of his close presence. The effect riveted me as a preteen; I was drawn to the vastness of the sky's radiance, assuring myself, "The God who created this gorgeous sunset sees insignificant me."

Though I had been told repeatedly that I was worthless, I sensed I was special to him. In the orchard, I always pictured Africa at the end of the sunset. That was when God first spoke to me about going to Africa as a missionary.

At age seventeen, I "ran away" from my abuse by attending college. As a freshman, I began dating a fine young man, Lon Tuin, who also spoke about missionary work. Lon and I were married a year later. God soon blessed our home with Jon, two years later with Jil, and Ronda eight years later.

As we raised our children, the thoughts of ministry in Africa faded. We sensed we were on the mission field in America, living in a multicultural, socioeconomically diverse community. Lon became a high school teacher and then a guidance counselor. I eventually completed my bachelor of arts in education, which allowed me to substitute teach. When Jon entered college, I went on to attain my California teaching credential, which enabled me to teach elementary school full time. Life was busy and bustling, and we felt God's blessing.

As I look back, I can see how God knew I was not then suited to serve as a missionary to Africa. I had too many issues to confront before I would feel whole and ready to help others on the opposite side of the world. Those around me did not realize the extent of my periodic horrifying and obsessive thoughts, depression, and insecurities—the results of abuse.

People thought of me as a happy person. And God did help me to enjoy my family and be professionally productive and active in the community and church. God also knew that those dark periods were preparing me for unexpected service later in life. When I was forty, a tragedy directly affected our lives, and the black cloud of depression threatened to smother me. I sought pastoral counseling, and that is when the nightmare began. What should have been a healing experience, became abuse.

Two years later, I wrote my story, *What about Her: A True Story of Clergy Abuse Survival.* Soon after its publication in 1997, I was asked to assume the directorship of Tamar's Voice, a ministry to help women abused by a member of the clergy. For the past eighteen years, Lon and I have been able to help scores of women (and husbands) all around the world find healing from the destruction of clergy abuse.

In the late spring of 2012, I received an email from Pastor Paul Odari in Kenya. Could I speak at their August conference for abused women? I responded, "Oh, I can't come! It is too short of notice. Besides, I am too old!" Yet I continued to communicate with Pastor Paul, even as I kept wondering, "Can I trust this man?" His webpage and online chats—all seemed to support a trustworthy story. I let my guard down enough to continue our dialogue, and I discussed the details with our son Jon and his wife, Heather. When they came from Chicago to our home in Indiana that Christmas, we talked more about the Kenyan opportunity with Divine Life Ministries under the leadership of Pastors Paul and Mary. One morning, Jon asked, "Mom, what is keeping you from going to see them?"

"Well, I am afraid. I don't think it would be wise for your dad to go because of his health. I am certainly not going to go alone. . . . I am just too old!"

"What if Heather and I escort you? We could bring Ty," they said, referring to their oldest child who is a professional videographer. "He could make a documentary of the trip."

At that moment, I knew I was going to Kenya! God reminded me of the call planted in my heart as a teenager. Now, at the age of seventy-two, I heard him whisper, "Now is the time!" I thought of Joseph in the Bible. He was mistreated, yet God spared him to save the nation of Israel. God told him, "What was meant for evil, I used for good" (Gen. 50:20, my paraphrase). My suffering was not in vain; God allowed me to go through the tragic experiences to prepare me for this moment. I would be there to comfort hurting women in the same manner God has comforted me (see 2 Cor. 1:4).

Pastor Paul is a passionate, visionary man who believes that Africa can be changed as women are empowered. His mother experienced extreme abuse by her first husband before he left her with five children, no home, and no means to provide. She married again to a responsible man who was killed when Paul was only ten years old. Paul's mother and siblings were left destitute and became homeless, living in the bush. Paul spoke of how vulnerable and afraid he felt, with no roof and walls to protect them.

He told us of his vision to have a "rescue home" for women like his mother and her children. He believes strongly that abused women need a place to heal; even more, they need a place to become empowered so they can learn to sustain themselves and their children.

During our time in the village of Sikhendu, Kenya, we witnessed the strong church and charitable ministries of Pastor Paul and Mary—a thriving church leadership training program, weekly home church groups, Saturday evangelistic crusades in outlying villages, a program feeding homeless children, and an elementary school.

We decided Paul was "the real deal." Paul, Mary, and their children have become our Kenyan children and grandchildren. We have become their "Mai" and "Baba." We talk to them every other day via the Internet, and our bonds continue to strengthen.

God has called me to help them build the Tamar's Women Rescue Centre in Kenya.[1] We helped them purchase land and they are building a facility and program to meet the needs of twenty mothers and their children. All of this is in conjunction with Paul and Mary.

Now, in the sunset of my life, I feel the sun rising within the sunset. God has lit a new passion within me, one that fuels my relentless persistence. I thank him for this opportunity to fulfill the African call. I hope, before I view my final sunset, to visit a completed Tamar's Women Rescue Centre in Kenya.

None of us need to experience oppression and abuse in order to fight bullies and abusers, or to stand in the gap for their victims. But because of these experiences, God has helped revive in me the energy of my youth. Now, within each sunset, I cannot wait to see his sunrise.

NOTE

1. For more information about Tamar's Voice and Tamar's Women Rescue Centre, visit www.tamarsvoice.org.

MORE THAN A COINCIDENCE

DEBBY MACK (WITH TONY MACK)

Editor's Note: Some friends simply can't hide in a room. Their personalities and profiles won't let them. Tony and Debby Mack have that handsome and beautiful combination working. They're laid back but could pass for celebrities. Tony is tall, with extremely broad shoulders, and if you're around long enough you'll learn they're the huggin' kind. The Macks are one of the couples I always seem to notice in our expansive sanctuary, predictably down on the far right. He's usually in a suit, and she's always accented by coiffed hair and a Marie Osmond smile. They also are that couple many aspire to be, happy with just being together. Tony has battled some health issues, and none with more awareness of mortality than the one they share with us below. It hits on a subject that, at times, consume us: death.

The original draft was considerably longer with attention to many more details. It revealed just how frozen in memory the events below are for the Macks, and understandably so. The following, with their approval, is a shorter version that captures the journey to and from death's door. It also begs another question, who will die first, my spouse, closest friends, or me? This story arrived days before the passing of one of my author friends. In that case, he was also with his wife, and she also did everything possible to save him, and then some. But in the end, God took him home. These are mysterious matters, but they also provoke our deepest curiosities about our will and fight to live and our efforts to help others do the same—and, if it's not being trite, to realize life and death is a matter of God's timing.

❧ ❧ ❧

"Friday the thirteenth" is a phrase that movies have forged into fictional lore, but for our family a Friday episode actually took a scary turn. Tony hit the ground hard, and it should have been a telltale sign that all was not well with my fun-loving husband. Our family chef, he fainted while cooking. Tony immediately rebounded and seemed fine, working and playing with our two little granddaughters. Then Sunday morning came, and our world changed. "Friday's here but Sunday's coming" took on a whole new and contrary meaning.

We had overslept, and while snuggling as we awoke he distinctly said he'd slept like a baby. Those were his last words before turning deep purple. He had just rolled over and let out all his breath in one strange gurgling sound. Urgency eclipsed serenity.

I jumped up to check for a pulse and breath. He had neither. What I thought was a heart attack was later diagnosed as sudden cardiac death. The time on the alarm clock was just before 9:00 a.m. I suppose people recall some of the most random things in crisis.

I screamed to rouse our son, Chad, and he found the cell phone and called 911 while I started CPR on Tony. I hadn't practiced for years, but I remembered enough to do chest compressions and rescue breathing—a lot easier on the practice mannequin. The clock now read 9:10, and I was in some level of shock. I thought I had really lost my husband but kept working on him anyway. Throughout the ordeal I kept crying out to God and talking to Tony.

Finally, around 9:20, I sensed a change in Tony. I did CPR a couple more times, then Tony opened his eyes, looking wild eyed and frightened.

When the EMTs arrived, Tony was disoriented. After recapping what had just happened, they asked Tony if he wanted to go with them. It seemed a strange question since he had been dead for twenty minutes, but was now alive.

He just held up his index finger and said over and over, "Minute, minute, minute, guys," as if he was asking for time. And then a numbing series of mandatory questions followed. His name and the day? He got those right. Was he going with them or staying home? He just stared at them. They asked him again. This time he said he was staying home. I begged the ambulance crew for time to help Tony understand. They had to go and asked Tony to sign a paper. Then they were gone. Tony doesn't remember them.

I kept telling him what had happened, but it didn't register. I said he needed to go to the hospital, but he decided to take a shower! I called family members, and several came. Our daughter, Tiffany, couldn't believe we hadn't left for the hospital yet, and she called the county ambulance. Tony remembers having me tell them we were going to drive ourselves.

When we walked out to the car, Tony headed for the driver's seat until my sister, Pam, reminded him that, if the roles were reversed, he wouldn't want me to drive myself. Though I kept reminding him what had happened, he couldn't remember.

When we got to the ER, the medical staff was astounded by Tony's condition and put him in ICU. Twice in the first twenty-four hours, he went into ventricular tachycardia: a very dangerous rhythm. During the second episode, he "coded"—near death. The doctors said he was probably in tachycardia several minutes before his sudden cardiac death at home.

On Monday morning, Tony was rapidly retaining fluid and struggling for breath with a very high heart rate and extremely low blood pressure. They inverted his bed to raise his blood pressure, but doing so also made breathing harder. I sat by his bed all night, afraid to close my eyes. Our small hospital wanted to lifeline Tony to the Heart Center, a top-notch, private hospital in Carmel, Indiana, but weren't sure it was possible since it took few Medicaid patients, such as Tony. But God opened that door—and a bed!

Tony's departure on that transport was the hardest moment of my life. After various visitors prayed, Tony said good-bye to Tiffany, then to me, assuring me of his love forever. He wanted to leave nothing unsaid.

I was afraid to enter his new room, unsure what I'd find. But there he was, looking better and joking with the nurses! He recalled feeling horrible during the transport before accidentally spilling a whole cup of ice water on his chest. It might be a corny metaphor, but Tony felt God was covering him with love, just like the ice water. Soon after we arrived, we met Pastor Ted and Lynn, who prayed with us and offered their home for lodging.

Tuesday morning, Tony had a heart catheterization. The good news: zero blockages or he likely would have died a long time ago. The bad news: a critically enlarged heart. The long vigil began; family members arrived. I didn't sleep for three days. I made the hour-long trip home to tend to necessities, but I couldn't sleep in our bedroom.

Hope dissipated once I returned to the hospital; Tony's kidneys were failing along with his liver and spleen. Mom put Tony on prayer chains, and more family members arrived to pray. One night, with my dad beside him, we had a God moment. Tony had been having trouble sleeping because of fluid in his lungs and nonfunctioning kidneys, but during Dad's prayer, he fell asleep. Later, he began using the bathroom again.

Such mundane daily tasks become monumental achievements.

The liver and kidneys, doctors decided, were in system shock from his organs going so long without adequate circulation during the Sunday ordeal. They predicted his organs would recover, and within a few days they did.

Tony's main surgery was originally planned for Friday, but since his platelet count kept going down and his water weight kept going up, they decided to reschedule for Monday—though it would eventually be postponed four times, total. Tony's heart had atrial fibrillation, an incorrect beat in the upper chambers, and the left ventricle was getting no signal, causing blood to pool in his heart. The plan was to implant a device to keep his heart in rhythm.

They hoped that with the devices, Tony's heart might heal faster and function more normally. They said the plan could "buy him a chunk of time" before a transplant was required. He needed as much time as possible, because the transplant doctor said Tony had to lose fifty more pounds just to get on the transplant list. With twenty-nine pounds gained in water weight in nine days, this was a challenge. Tony often sat on the edge of his bed at night just to catch his breath.

On Sunday we had a little worship service in his room with Tony's sisters, and my mom. During another God moment my sister shared a verse where she had flipped open her Bible. She believed it was Tony's verse—Psalm 118:17: "I shall not die, but live, and declare the works of the LORD" (KJV).

Atnal fibrillation was damaging Tony's heart, so the doctors wanted to shock it back to normal beat. His heart was so bad that it was very risky, but necessary to buy more time. As they prepared the equipment, I overheard one doctor say, "This is a very critical patient. I'm not sure he can handle it, but it's his best chance." It's hard to capture the intensity of prayer while they worked on him, but I was elated when the doctors informed me that the procedure had worked on the first attempt!

After the procedure, they increased Tony's diuretic, allowing him to lose fluid, first one pound, then eight in one day, finally losing thirty-two pounds in a week. The fluid retention no longer posed a detriment to surgery, but his low platelet count did. Finally, doctors determined he was sensitive to blood thinners and discontinued them. Monday morning, with his platelet count at normal levels, they said yes to his morning surgery to implant the device. The surgeon spoke with us, telling us that it could take three to seven hours, there was a 20 to 30 percent chance of failure, and a possibility Tony could die in surgery.

As we gathered in the waiting room, among tears and prayers, Pastor Ted walked in, bringing hugs and more prayers. We'd been there about two and a half hours when they called us back to Tony's room. What? So soon? I was alarmed until the doctor walked in, smiling. "It was perfect!" he said. "We set a new record for time. And your husband serenaded us on his way into the operating room."

Later, Tony said it was like singing while heading into battle. He even got to pray and witness with the surgical team.

The plan was to send us home on Thursday, because everything was working beautifully—so beautifully, in fact, that I spent Wednesday night visiting a longtime friend, in town for a conference. But when I returned on Thursday morning, Tony had a pained look on his face and a five-pound sandbag on his shoulder. His platelets had dropped again. He had spontaneous internal bleeding around his implant, and the sandbag was applying pressure to slow the bleeding. With this new bleeding, the plans changed again. We had to stay longer, while Tony received platelet transfusions for three days.

By Sunday they said he could go home and have outpatient testing. That afternoon, I packed everything in the car. (You accumulate a lot in three weeks!) A staff member helped Tony in, and we were on our way. Having him sitting beside me felt wonderful—almost like a dream.

God promises never to leave us or forsake us. We knew God was with Tony—with all of us—through those days. But I know God still would've been with me even if Tony hadn't come back home that morning.

God has shown us how wonderful our friends and family are, and most of all how wonderful he is. We've witnessed God's omnipotence, love, and willingness to intervene. Does God still heal? Absolutely! He rejoices in meeting his children's needs. But how often do we fail to receive what he longs to provide because we don't ask?

Looking back, we see God's provision everywhere. We see it in the then new extra-firm mattress (instead of our previous waterbed) that our family had given us for Christmas; making CPR possible. We see it in the spilled ice water he used to encourage Tony; in Ted and Lynn who opened their home; in the support and love that paid our bills when Tony wasn't able to work; and in God's presence and blessing whenever we worshiped together in that hospital room.

We know God has a purpose in all he does. We don't know what the future holds, but God has given us this time together, and we are grateful for every day. We are truly blessed and will never be the same again, praising God every day, as we "live, and declare the works of the LORD" (Ps. 118:17 KJV).

BLESSED BY ADVERSITY

MARCIA WOODARD

Editor's Note: *I think most of us find it hard to relate to other people's dreams—not dreams for one's vocation, but the bizarre kind we enter when we doze off. We've all had them, and I hope we always will. You'll be the judge of where the following story lands on your scale of the fantastic, but it's one that Marcia says is from God. Before discarding the merit of dreams or visions, look at the biblical story of Joseph in prison with the baker or Peter's vision of assorted animals (see Gen. 40 and Acts 10:9–23). And dreams continued to play a significant role in the early church and then beyond. St. Augustine's mother placed considerable merit in them.*

There's another dimension to Marcia's story: the quest for a spiritual awakening and one's deep desire for excitement about life and faith. We might call it spiritual zeal. We know that some spiritual leaders, like Billy Sunday and D. L. Moody, seemed to thrive on emotional energy. Moody went so far as to say, "I'd rather have zeal without knowledge than knowledge without zeal."[1] Of course, God doesn't require us to make a choice, but Moody's penchant for overstatement drives home the point. The apostle Paul challenges us not to let our zeal be lacking (see Rom. 12:11).

The following is a very transparent look into a friend's life, sharing an otherworldly moment, so to speak, and the very hues of her personal fiber. It was hard for me not to think of The Boy in the Bubble *and* The Truman Show, *when she introduces the bubble imagery. Imagery and the fantastic have special force when they prompt reflection on the real. This story made me think, as well, about the Holy Spirit's role in our joy. I happened to be reading Jim Cymbala's* Fresh Wind, Fresh Fire *while editing this chapter, which prompted such a thought.*

I'm not sure how you deal with people's transparency, but like Marcia's journey, that's between you and God. This is one of those stories that will likely follow you to solitary places. So I leave you here to read and to ask yourself important questions: "Do I believe that God speaks in such dreams or visions?" "Am I excited about my faith?" "Can I fathom the extent of God's love? "Why?" or "Why not?"

▼　▼　▼

I tend to be an emotional person. That is, both my feelings and hunches drive many decisions. Maybe it's just a bent toward visceral decision making when my gut feelings prove dominant. Conversely, discouragement surfaces when I don't feel well, emotionally or physically. For a long time, that emotional base didn't form a very stable foundation for my spiritual journey. If I felt good or happy, then it was easy to believe that God loved me. It was easy to follow him.

However, if I got sick or had an argument (especially with someone I loved), then I'd get discouraged. It seemed as if I'd let God down and he couldn't really love me. I just felt like that annoying neighbor kid who is your child's best friend, the one your patience barely survives. In my summary of divine relationships, I knew Jesus loved me, but God the Father, on the other hand, merely tolerated me.

During that dark season of my adulthood, God always felt disappointment, disapproval, and annoyance toward me; or so I thought. When I was less than the perfect mom, I felt guilty and grew even grumpier. In some convoluted reasoning at the time, it seemed God's annoyance with me made me more annoyed with my kids. I'd skip Sunday church at times because I was tired. It was cyclical, of course, as I'd then want to avoid him the next Sunday. Feeling discouraged and depressed, I'd assume he was disappointed with me for feeling that way, which made me even more discouraged and depressed. But I just kept plugging along.

Have you ever just wanted someone's approval? Looking back, I realize I had it from the very people I cared the most about—but I felt no glimmer of affirmation in that self-imposed "bleak house" season. I didn't feel like I could please God, and I increased my drudgery by worrying about what other people thought of me. Were they watching me? Were they laughing at me behind my back? How could I make them like me? Make them think I was cool? Make them want me for a friend?

My audience was more than family and friends. It often included strangers—and I used their approval, along with those closer to me, as the gauge of my worth. Because there were always people in the audience who didn't seem to approve, I never felt very worthwhile.

Eventually I grew tired of the emotional roller coaster. I wasn't sure what the answer was, and I clearly didn't have it, but I'd had enough of the continual on again/off again: God loves me; God loves me not. "They" love me; "they" love me not. I didn't want to waste any more time wavering.

I prayed, "God, I'm following you no matter what. I will do what you want me to, regardless of how I feel."

What happened next? Nothing! For twelve months, I felt nothing. I sensed nothing. In the past, I had read my Bible, prayed, and attended church for the good feeling I got from participating. Now I did them purely out of commitment. No warm fuzzies. No emotional reward. They weren't superficial activities; they were intentional actions done to maintain my relationship with God, no matter what I felt or didn't feel.

After a year of pure obedience reflecting my best efforts, my faith gained new strength and grew new roots, but with no emotional lift. As you might imagine, I longed for the emotional joy as well as the cognitive. It wasn't a craving for emotions to live and die by, but to have as an added dimension. I wanted to know God heard me when I prayed.

On one Sunday morning, I got ready for church and left our kids in the other room with my husband while I went to be alone with God.

Lying on the bed in my Sunday best, I tried to pray. It seemed pointless. Every word I uttered seemed to bounce off the ceiling and land with a thud on the floor. I began to feel a desperation for God, like Jacob wrestling with the angel or David lamenting in the Psalms.

I prayed again, but with a different tenor: "God, I will stay here until I know you have heard me!" Because I had been experiencing such an emotional dry spell in my spiritual life, I fully expected to spend hours, if not days, waiting for God to appear. But after what seemed like only an instant, I sensed God there with me, and he unfolded a vision.

The ceiling disappeared from the room, and the roof had lifted from the house. The sky was crisp blue and breathtaking. Then, in the vision, the atmosphere vanished, and I could see deep into space, with millions of stars. Still in the vision, God showed me what it would be like to float up, out of the walls of the house, up through the sky, up higher and higher, out into space among the stars, out of sight of the earth.

There I floated in space: quiet, peaceful, unafraid, and surrounded by stars. Suspended there, I realized that I was inside a giant, transparent, golden bubble. I could see and hear everything outside the bubble, but I was completely enclosed and sheltered.

I didn't know what the bubble was, or how I felt about it, so I began to explore it. I couldn't see any door or opening, which made me wonder: can I get out or am I trapped? I floated my way to the side of the bubble, where I could touch its golden "skin" and try to learn about it.

I tried pinching it, tugging it, pushing it, and poking it, but I couldn't tear it or make any opening in it. I noticed an asteroid nearby and wanted to see it up closer. By paddling with my hands and kicking with my feet, I was able to float in its direction. The bubble traveled with me, keeping me enveloped and secure. I was still puzzled, still poking and pinching at the bubble's surface, trying to make an opening. The skin of the bubble was strong but flexible. Although I could stretch it and move it, I could not escape from it.

Finally, puzzled and a little frustrated, I said aloud to myself, "What is this thing?" Immediately, I sensed God saying, "It's my love. You did nothing to put yourself inside it, but it keeps you safe and protected, while letting you choose what you do and where you go. And regardless of where you go or what you do, you will never be outside my love. My love will never let you go!"

At that instant, I was back on earth, in my house, lying on my bed, still in my church clothes. Everything was the same, but . . . God loved me! I knew he loved me! I picked up my Bible to see if it looked different now that it was a letter from someone who loved me. It was different! I flipped open to Psalm 139 and read verse 8: "If I ascend up into heaven, thou art there: if I make my bed in hell, behold, thou art there" (KJV).

God not only loved me, but he was also with me! A God who would stay by my side in the hell of depression wouldn't leave me—ever! I no longer have to live cringing from one moment to the next trying to earn God's approval, afraid of losing it or bracing for his annoyance and disapproval. God loves me, and he's my only true audience, the only one whose acceptance I truly need. That frees me to love others, because I don't need their approval. I can just reach out and share God's love with them.

Of course, some days, I forget he's my audience of one. That's why he's put a reminder in the sky. In Sunday school, the kids learn how the rainbow is visible in the clouds as a symbol that God keeps his promises. But one rainy day, God showed me an extra reminder at the end of a rainbow. Someday when you see an especially bright rainbow, look carefully just below it and you might see what looks like a big, transparent golden bubble. For me, it's God's reminder that his promises are based on his inexhaustible love for us.

Be Transformed

Also as eBooks!

SoulShift
The Measure of a Life Transformed

Steve DeNeff and David Drury offer an approach to spiritual transformation which focuses less on measuring how much time we are spending on spiritual inputs and more on measuring who we are becoming in Christ.

ISBN: 978-0-89827-697-8
eBook ISBN: 978-0-89827-599-5

FaultLines
Challenges that Transform Your Soul

Steve DeNeff reveals to both the young and veteran in faith how soul-growing transformations happen only as God breaks through spiritual hardness.

ISBN: 978-0-89827-926-9
eBook ISBN: 978-0-89827-927-6